Total School Mis-management

A Step-by-Step Guide to Creating
Chaos in Schools
by David E. Hellawell

QUESTIONS PUBLISHING COMPANY

The articles collected in this book were first published between 1990 and 1994 in the magazines *School Governor* and *Managing Schools Today* published by The Questions Publishing Company Ltd, 27 Frederick Street, Hockley, Birmingham B1 3HH.

ISBN: 1 898149 31 3

Acknowledgements
The publishers are grateful to the following for their work on this book:
Iqbal Aslam
Pamela Hopkinson
Liz John
Mark Townsend

Designed and typeset by: The Questions Publishing Company
Printed by Redwood Books

To Barbara with thanks for all her help.

ABOUT THE AUTHOR

David Hellawell taught modern languages for eight years in secondary schools. During over 25 years in teacher education and training he has had experience of teaching and learning at all levels. He is currently Associate Dean and Professor of Education at the University of Central England in Birmingham. His PhD thesis was on headteacher appraisal. He is Past President of the Association for Teacher Education in Europe (ATEE) and was the Founding President of the Permanent Liaison Committee of European Associations in Education (PLEASE). He has acted as a consultant in education management for various organisations and official bodies including the Commission of the European Union. He is still working out what he wants to be when he grows up.

ACKNOWLEDGEMENTS

I would like to thank Howard Sharron and Liz John for their help and encouragement over the years with *School Governor* and *Managing Schools Today*. I hereby forgive them for the editorial butchery they have frequently committed on the highly implausible grounds of lack of space. My thanks also to Iqbal Aslam for his splendid cartoons.

CONTENTS

PREFACE

The articles gathered in this collection were written for *School Governor* and its successor magazine *Managing Schools Today*. They are all on the overall theme of managing (or mismanaging) in the world of education.

I have been a manager in education in the formal sense ever since what now seems the tender age of 25 when I was designated the head of a German department in the grammar school in which I first taught. Since then I have filled various fulltime managerial posts in comprehensive schools, in colleges of education, in a polytechnic and in a university. The last few institutional transformations, together with the concomitant changes in managerial role, were achieved by the subtle strategy of staying in the same organisation as it passed from one metamorphosis to another. This is known in the trade as masterly inactivity. In addition to this, I have occupied my copious leisure time with a variety of other recognised managerial activities inside and outside education.

The key word in the last sentence is "recognised". In fact most of us are unrecognised managers for much of our waking lives. Anyone who tells me that a parent running a home, for example, is not a manager is, in my view, talking rubbish. Certainly I hold firmly to the view that all teachers are managers no matter what their official titles in school may be. Teachers are there to manage pupils' learning, and that is an onerous and complex managerial activity. (It can, of course, also be fascinating and rewarding, but that's also true of most other managerial activities on a good day.)

The number of people engaged in management in schools these days is expanding all the time as governors and parents play increasing roles under the government legislation which has poured out at an unprecendented rate of knots (in every sense of the word) in recent years. The old cliché that governors govern and heads manage should have been buried a long time ago. Heads must feel from time to time these days that everyone under the sun manages, but it's they who carry the can if managerial disasters ensue.

In most of these articles, I have attempted to write, at least in part, in a humorous style. One relatively easy way to do this is to demonstrate how easy it is to be a catastrophically bad manager by doing all the wrong things in the wrong ways; or even some of the right things in the wrong ways. This technique has the added advantage that you can counter the all too prevalent tendency to present management as some sort of ideal blueprint activity where all is for the best in the best of all possible worlds. This gives an air of blatant unreality to far too many of the writings on management in all spheres. Furthermore, too many managers have believed their own propaganda by acting out the managerial role in ways which are often simultaneously pompous, serious, self-righteous and solemn. This air of gravitas makes it all the funnier to expose the reality behind the rhetoric. Many TV sitcoms follow in the glorious tradition of Groucho Marx and his brothers in basing their humour on the ludicrous gap between the smart public front of management and its rough and exposed backside.

It is precisely because too many managers have a hyper-rational view of the world that (a) they are under unnecessary stress for too much of the time, and (b) their various come-uppances can be so funny. The world is far funnier than most management textbooks allow, and the average manager is more fallible and less prescient than they tend to assume. The question Woody Allen posed some years ago: "How do you make God laugh?", has in his own life now had the answer confirmed: "Show him your plans". This is why many managers need to be devious and cunning merely to survive. Ducking and weaving become second nature even if they are not talents acquired in the cradle.

It isn't just in education that managerial foul-ups occur. One of my most heart-warming moments was when one of my bolshier ex-students came back to see me one day long after throwing up his embryonic pedagogic career to work for one of our larger industrial concerns as a trainee manager. His opening words were more or less to the effect that he took back all the unkind things he had ever said about the college because compared to his new employers we were shining paragons of managerial virtue. The subsequent decline of this nameless company would tend to suggest you did not have to be Sir John Harvey Jones to detect flaws in its management systems. The fact that the college in which I was then earning a humble crust has long since perished is, of course, another matter entirely.

The alert reader will have spotted that I used the translated words of Voltaire in a completely unattributed fashion some three paragraphs ago. I see no reason for him to turn in his grave on that account because he was only satirising the ideas of someone else at the time anyway. One of the greatly liberating aspects, for someone otherwise engaged in the groves of aca-deme, in writing what another writer used to refer to as *feuilletons,* or comic essays of this kind, is that you do not feel obliged to search out references and write down endless foot-notes and bibliographies etc. In other words, you can cheerfully borrow ideas from a variety of literary and non-literary sources on a non-attributable basis on the grounds that you are trying to amuse readers not grind them into the academic dust. I do want, however, to underline the fact that these articles are based upon an understanding of the theory and practice of management in education which, despite its undoubted imperfections, has, nevertheless been built up over more than thirty years of listening to and reading the ideas of others. The fact that most of these sources go unrecorded in articles of this type does not mean that I am not aware of the debts these writings must owe to those sources, both consciously and unconsciously.

I must also stress the fact that all names of characters who crop up in these squibs have been changed to protect the guilty. Any of my friends who find their own names cropping up in various inept guises should console themselves with the thought that these were simply the first names beyond my own that came to mind when I was thinking up fictional *noms-de-guerre* for the great managerial cock-ups of our time. The trouble with this game is that nobody believes the wildly improbably coincidences that can occur in these respects. I actually wrote the Abominable No Man chapter (page 11) weeks before John Patten referred to a group of parents, whose views were slightly different from his own, as "Neanderthal". The fact that I had already given the very common forename of John to an imaginary backwoods politician I had called Neanderthalman in that vignette was one of those acts of serendipity which suggest that there may be a deity who has a sense of humour after all. (Indeed, since I first wrote that last sentence, the reference to "John Neanderthalman of the Back to Basics party" has taken on added significance.)

Finally, a letter of intended praise from a reader of one of my polemics suggests that there is a need for a last word of caution. Because I am attempting to castigate bad management in as sardonic a fashion as possible, it does not follow that I am attacking managerial theory and practice in general. This would not only be to snarl ungratefully at the sources of income by which I keep my family in the style to which it has become accustomed (i.e. genteel shabbiness), but to undermine the essential message I am trying to convey. This is that for the good of us all we should be constantly striving to improve the way we manage education, and that one way to do this is to try to identify the dross of bad managerial practice and to hold it up to public ridicule.

THE ABOMINABLE
NO MAN

Any quick flip through the books and articles on management in education will soon show you that most writers about schools still use the terms 'administrator', 'manager' and 'leader' more or less indiscriminately, as though they were, in effect, synonyms. Yet, in my view, there is considerable illumination to be generated by differentiating sharply between them.

I would argue that while it is theoretically possible for one individual to combine a perfect balance of the qualities of the administrator, the manager and the leader, it is, in reality, highly unlikely that this will be the case. The psychological characteristics of a typical administrator, for example, will usually be found to differ markedly from those of a typical manager as I shall go on to define these categories. My basic contentions are that most effective organisations need all three categories operating on their behalf; that schools are no exception to the rule; and that no organisation should expect the same individual to combine equally the vices and virtues of all three categories. If my arguments to support these contentions seem sound, then the corollary is that all institutions need organisational teams which comprise individuals who are primarily administrators, managers or leaders.

To begin with administrators, I would define these as individuals whose major organisational purpose in life is to maintain the status quo. As Sir Humphrey Appleby has so ably demonstrated to us throughout series of *Yes Minister* and *Yes Prime Minister*, the most damning word in the mouth of the administrator is 'novel'. If an administrator describes a proposed project as 'novel', it means that he or she regards it as just slightly less dangerous than Chernobyl the night before the cock-up. A novel idea is likely to set a precedent. Any precedent contains within itself, by definition, an element of risk. Therefore, novelty is to be avoided, because the last thing the administrator wants to do in this life, or probably during the next three reincarnations, is to take a risk. Risk avoidance is what administration is all about.

With all due respect to Sir Humphrey's creators, the greatest chronicler of the supreme ability of the administrator to avoid almost all positive decision-making remains the C. Northcote Parkinson of *Parkinson's Law*. 'Decision-making', by this definition, means actually supporting something or somebody calculated to change the status quo. In fact, of course, opposing any change to the status quo is in itself just as much a decision as support for change would be, but nobody, least of all the administrator, usually notices this. As Reich's Second Law states: "Administration is neutral in favour of the present policy."

Parkinson identifies the true administrator as the Abominable No Man. Saying yes to a novel idea associates the administrator with the risks which surely lie ahead, "but saying no is relatively safe. It requires no explanation because no action follows... He cannot be held responsible for any failure and will not be asked to aid in insuring success. Few will remember his opposition and those who do can be told that the plan in its original form was impractical and that its effective application after revision owed much to the process of healthy criticism to which it was sub-jected in the early stages of its development. The No Man has little to lose." By this stage, the reader may well be asking the obvious question. If this is the nature of the administrator, why do schools need them? My response to this would be that in some respects there are few organisations, which, on the one hand, are more conservative than schools. The staffs of schools should not primarily be held responsible for this state of affairs. If we have to seek scapegoats, let's start with the politicians, and then go on to the parents. As any quick scan of the tabloid press will tell you, most politicians are fond of recalling the golden age of education of their youth. If only traditional values had been held on to; if only corporal punishment had been re-tained; if only the basic subjects in the curriculum were taught as they used to be taught etc., then this proud nation state of ours would still be as it was a half century or so ago. The impli-cation is that we would again be winning the Battle of El Ala-mein or whichever 50th anniversary happens to be appropriate.

What these politicians do not appear to have noticed is that following this argument to its logical conclusion, we should have been fighting Rommel's tanks with the long bow which had been so successful at Agincourt. As it so happens, this time round we're in competition with the Deutschemark, which is why the school curriculum and everything else has to come in line with the modern world for us just to stay in the same place. (Actually the chance of staying in the same place as far as the conversion rate of the pound sterling to the Deutschemark of my youth would be a fine thing.) Why do politicians talk this kind of drivel? Because they are, in fact, rational human beings who are unusually adept at saying the kinds of things that they think are likely to win them votes at the next election.

Who are these folks, then, that so like to hear this abject twaddle that they are likely to put their X on their ballot paper alongside candidate John Neanderthalman (Back to Basics Party)? These, dear readers, are the average parents of the kiddywinkies in your school. No-one is more reactionary than the average parent. If it was good enough for them it must be good enough for Jimmy and Jenny. What's more, how are Jimmy and Jenny going to stay dependent on their mums and dads if the latter can't actually understand the homework their offspring have to do these days, let alone do it for them? Indeed, there is an obvious correlation between these changes in the nature of homework and the rising incidence of drug-taking among the young. Should any smart Alec academic try to confuse the issue by suggesting that correlations tell you nothing at all about cause and effect, it's obvious he or she should be taken down a peg or two.

Perhaps I exaggerate ever so slightly to make my point, but the point remains valid. There is an enormous amount of public pressure for schools to stay the same. Any change is likely to be labelled as 'progressive', and you can't be more damning than that. (At precisely the same time, however, these very same parents and politicians will be pressing schools and their staffs to stay abreast of the times in which we live. More of this anon. All I need to point out at this juncture, is that it is this kind of doublethink on the part of the adult punters that makes managing schools so entertaining an occupation.)

Under these circumstances it is essential to have some administrators in schools. Equally, for reasons I will go into in detail later, administrators should, under no circumstances, now be allowed to pretend they are school leaders. School leaders, however, need to have these men and women around them who will take care of the large amounts of routine work which remains much the same week in, week out and indeed year in, year out. Administrators love this kind of routine. Concentrating on the minute routine details is a wonderful defence mechanism against having to take account of the really big changes which are for ever unfortunately occurring around them. This routine detail confirms to them what they have always known, namely that the world is essentially unchanging and that they have made an invaluable contribution to keeping it like this. If only those managers and leaders didn't keep on trying to change things, this would be quite a good world in which to live.

Of course, administrators *do* make very valuable contributions to school life in many respects. In my experience, the real school leaders have very low boredom thresholds indeed. If they were not continually thwarted and frustrated by the administrators, then a life working for and with these leaders would be too fascinating for words. It must have been a Chinese administrator, and not a leader, who first voiced the curse that his or her enemy should live in interesting times.

Actually, administrators never flourished as luxuriantly at the school level as at the education 'office' level in some of the most hidebound of the LEAs. At this level the maintenance of the status quo had become an art form. The four key rules by which this game was played by the local government administrators concerned were formulated long ago and far away by a certain Dr. Sharu S. Rangnekar, but they are still totally applicable in the current UK context.
1. If you can avoid a decision, do so.
2. If you can avoid a decision, don't delay it.
3. If you can get somebody else to avoid a decision, don't avoid it yourself.
4. If you cannot get one person to avoid the decision, appoint a committee.

In years gone by all the school administrator had to do was to utter the dread words: "I think we'll have to refer this one to the office." Once into the Local Education Authority maw, there was no way whatsoever that it could ever emerge as a live issue. Unfortunately for the administrator at the school level, the local management of schools and the increasing number of grant-maintained schools threaten to remove the excuse of the 'office' for ever. Furthermore, the imminent demise of the Local Education Authority, as we all knew and loved it, is actually strengthening the need for more managers and even leaders at the school level. Unlike administrators, both of these groups are not averse to dealing with change. Notwithstanding all that has been said in this article, change is increasingly the name of the game in schools, and you need people in place who actually want to play the game. Managers are, however, not necessarily, or even probably, the same as leaders in this context. The difference between these two categories is the subject of the next chapter.

THE RIGHT BALANCE

I n the previous chapter I defined administrators as individuals whose major organisational purpose in life is to maintain the status quo. However, both managers and leaders are usually more concerned with dealing with change in other ways than merely attempting to repress or suppress it. They do not regard change as an enemy to be attacked and slain at any price, but expect to be actively promoting it where it would appear to be in the best interests of the organisations they serve.

There is, by my definition however, still one vital area of difference between managers and leaders. Managers expect to initiate change within the existing organisational culture. Leaders are quite prepared, and usually appear only too willing, to oversee changes in the organisational culture itself or at least significant aspects of that culture. Defined in this way, it is possible for an individual to be seen as a leader figure while nevertheless lacking certain significant managerial skills. It is equally, if not more, likely that many a 'good' manager could be a relatively 'poor' leader. Obviously, it is possible to be both a manager and a leader. Most of us will, at times I guess, also step into the administrator role if it suits us to block some proposed change.

When I now go on to differentiate between these categories, I am doing so in the terms of what the sociologists call 'ideal types'. In other words, I am differentiating, for the purposes of analysis, categories which in real life are often inextricably mixed in the behaviour patterns of any individual with managerial responsibilities. The essential point is that it is not easy for any one individual to reconcile these different roles, and, crucially, that most of us are much happier operating in one of the roles rather than in the others. So from now on in this article, a word such as 'leader' should be read as referring to an individual who prefers to operate in that role.

Before I can pursue this distinction between managers and leaders, I probably also need to spell out what I mean by organisational culture. To use Schein's well known definition, for any given group or organisation that has had a substantial history, culture is "the pattern of basic assumptions that a given group has invented, discovered or developed in learning to cope with its problems of external adaptation and internal integration." Thus, what is meant by 'organisational culture' is a pattern of basic assumptions that have worked well enough to be considered valid and, therefore, taught, consciously or unconsciously, to new members of an organisation as the correct way to perceive, think and feel in relation to those problems. "This is the way things work around here."

It is my contention that managers, as defined in this article, are quite happy to work within an existing organisational culture, and that they tend to make changes within that structure only when they feel that something is going wrong. Their basic philosophy in this respect is very much: "If it ain't bust don't fix it." To hark back to the administrator for a moment, this latter type would spend a considerable time inventing ingenious arguments to the effect that it wasn't really bust at all, even if the pieces were all strewn out on the floor for all to see.

The manager will at least face up to the need for change when it stares him or her in the face that this particular aspect of the organisation is no longer functioning effectively. In my experience, however, some leaders will want to change things whether they are working or not. Furthermore, without fairly fundamental and radical changes to the organisational culture itself, a particular kind of leader will quickly become bored and, if somehow prevented from making those changes, will all too quickly move on to another organisation where the transformation game is a real possibility.

What distinguishes the leader from both the administrator and the manager is that the leader tends to be proactive while the other two tend to be reactive, although the reactions of these latter two categories to new problems will differ along the lines I have already outlined. It is the leader who is constantly looking ahead, not to what is but to what ought to be or even to what might be. This orientation towards the future, if it turns out later to be on the right lines, is what observers usually refer to as 'vision'. If it lands the organisation deep into trouble, it tends to have other labels than vision attached to it! However, when Robert Reich said that a leader's vision is "the grain of sand in the oyster, not the pearl" he had it about right to my way of thinking.

It is useful in my experience to distinguish sharply between those leaders who carry their vision around with them in the form of ready carved tablets of stone, and those leaders who are prepared to develop a shared vision within their organisations which arises out of the realities of the common problems most of the employees recognise they are facing. The development of this latter kind of shared vision requires a no less proactive stance on the part of the leader than does the former, but it does also involve a commitment to listening and to seeing the facilitation of change through others as more productive than the imposition of change on others. Whatever the leadership style, however, there is no doubt that most leaders will try to take the organisation into new territory or uncharted seas.

Those who seek a quiet life should avoid organisations with leaders at the helm. Alternatively, those who value a touch of democracy as well as a dash of adventure should try to ensure that they work in organisations which have administrators and managers who can effectively combine with the leader to produce a managerial team for all seasons. For, as I have already implied, some leaders can easily become monsters if there are inadequate checks and balances to their powers. Those working in cabinet with Churchill during World War II may have found his moods difficult at times, but they could always console themselves with the thought that their counterparts in the Hitler regime were having somewhat greater difficulties with a tyrant who gave a bad name, probably for all time, to what was then the equivalent word for leader in the German language. Indeed, the horrendous events at Waco in Texas recently are eerily reminiscent at the organisational level of the effects at national level in the Germany of 1944 of people following in fanatic fashion a leader who, to those outside the 'cult', appeared evil and probably insane.

If we examine, in this context, the proposition that effective managers are people who do things right, while good leaders are people who do the right things (to adapt an idea from Peter Drucker and others), then there are some interesting corollaries. This notion still leaves open the possibility, for example, that efficient managers can do the wrong things right. Few historians have doubted the excellence of Albert Speer's managerial capabilities on behalf of Hitler's malevolently misdirected war effort.

On the other hand, you are unlikely to be a good leader if you do the right things in the wrong ways. Maybe good leaders should guide their effective managers in the right directions and then let the latter do their efficient best. In the previous chapter I made the case for the administrator in the school system, and the case for the manager is much stronger. It is a truism to assert that the environment in which schools operate has always been ever-changing. School management teams worth their salt always knew that unless they made internal adaptations to match the external mutations they were going to see their organisations decline in their effectiveness. Their essential counter to the bureaucrat's desire to maintain the status quo is the old adage that you've got to change even to stay in the same place.

Change will inevitably bring problems along with it, but problem solving is what management is all about. The manager's approach to this problem solving has traditionally been to look for rational, logical solutions. Such solutions have, of course, often proved to be non-existent, because real-life problems are not the kinds of puzzles we confront in those computer games where we know that a solution exists somewhere if only we could find it! Three or four unavailing, but nonetheless carefully planned, attempts to avoid the potential explosion at stage 3 usually mean, in real life, that we then rapidly conclude that there is no logical solution out there at all, and we fall back on rule of thumb reactions.

These managerial reactions are usually in the direction of minimising the obvious risks and dangers, and it is on these occasions that managers frequently seem indistinguishable from administrators. The distinction is that the true administrator is now saying: "I told you so", for he or she will undoubtedly have counselled caution in advance by suggesting that the unknown path ahead looked highly dangerous. Intuition has to be constantly called upon by managers for precisely these reasons, but even then we will frequently make post-hoc rationalisations that suggest to all around us, and unfortunately sometimes to ourselves as well, that any success achieved was all a result of a cunning plan which could not be divulged in advance.

The dangers of believing our own propaganda are obvious but the advantages in persuading others to believe it are considerable. People like to believe that their managers are logical, rational creatures. They like to believe this particularly when they think that an impartial and dispassionate decision about any particular issue is bound to go in their favour! These considerations do not necessarily apply to leaders at all. Leaders can be high-risk gamblers who tend to regard caution as a bureaucratic disease. Even when their gambles have failed miserably in the past, such leaders will go on to the next adventure relatively unabashed. At the national level in the UK, Winston Churchill's bold ideas in World War II do not seem to have been in any way tempered by his disasters, e.g Gallipoli, on the military front in World War I.

Not surprisingly perhaps, the scope for headteachers to be genuine leaders, as defined here, has been somewhat limited in the state sector in recent decades. The headteacher in most cases could be regarded as the branch manager whose outfit's organisational culture was to a large extent dictated by the 'head office' at the LEA. From my arguments about the culture of many LEAs in my previous chapter on administrators and managers, the pressure exerted by such LEA officialdom was bound to be exerted towards a bureaucratic and administrative stance. Heads in the state sector who tried to buck the bureaucratic trend often ended up as notorious rather than celebrated; a legal footnote and a warning to others. It was usually only in the private sector that heads had the scope and the freedom to develop a very distinctive school culture through their own creative vision.

Some of these heads seem larger than life. They are colourful figures who create schools in their own image. Neill and Summerhill are synonymous to most people as are Arnold and Rugby, Thring and Uppingham etc. We should also, however, not forget that the fictional Squeers and Dotheboys Hall were based by Dickens on real life examples, and this is yet another warning that leadership can so very easily slide into petty despotism. We could now be entering an era where the scope for leadership in the state sector is going to be very much wider. Those who think that the undermining of the LEAs merely presages a new era in which schools will find themselves in a central government straitjacket are, in my view, wide of the mark, certainly as far as headteachers are concerned. There may well be a national curriculum framework, but the scope for a head to help to create a distinctive 'mission' for his or her school will be, in general, much increased.

Along with the managerial responsibilities which are being devolved from LEAs to schools, go the possibilities for the head to be more than just a manager. Charisma may now be due for a comeback at the headteacher level. Charismatic school leaders are not primarily concerned with making relatively minor adjustments within an existing culture. Unless that culture is proving to be manifestly successful, they will be determined to transform the school and make fundamental changes in its mission and its structure. They will also not feel that they must slavishly conform to the pressures exerted by the most conservative of their pupils' parents. Those pressures certainly exist, as I made clear in the previous chapter, but it is not just a cliché to assert that we do indeed live in an increasingly pluralist society. Some heads will experience this as a mass of conflicting pressures which make their jobs well-nigh intolerable. Others will see that it gives them the opportunity to listen to very differing views and then to steer in their own best judged direction. This is what leadership is all about.

After all, we did have a somewhat similar forerunner to the new breed of Grant Maintained Schools and City Technology Colleges etc. in the Direct Grant Schools, which were also schools receiving finance directly from central government and outside the control of LEAs. There were some notable heads in that sector who made national reputations for themselves by helping to create a very special, if not unique, ethos in their schools. Eric James at Manchester Grammar School immediately springs to mind. Within a very few years of his arrival at the school he had, for example, disbanded the preparatory schools which had provided those parents who could afford the fees with a 'favoured' route into the school for their offspring. As can be imagined, he did this in the teeth of some very fierce opposition from a powerful parental lobby. Manchester Grammar School did not become the nationally famous meritocratic school par excellence of its time without very strong leadership.

My own experience of MGS suggests that the 'chief', as he was significantly known, was not without his detractors, as well as his fervent admirers, both inside and outside the school. As his recent obituaries and the subsequent correspondence in the educational press suggest, such figures as Eric James are highly controversial in death as in life. Their innovations are revered by some and detested by others. The essential point is that they do need the space and the freedom to act as genuine leaders. Perhaps their time has come again. If so then this article has attempted to point up not only the positive, but also the negative potential of such a development.

HOW SUBORDINATES CAN DEMOTIVATE THEIR MANAGERS

There have always been heaps of texts on how managers should go about motivating their subordinates and the rate of production of such tomes appears, if anything, to have increased in recent years. However, there does appear to be a gap in the market because I have yet to find a book advising subordinates on how to motivate their managers. What must exist somewhere, although I have been unable to track it down, is a textbook on how subordinates can *demotivate* their managers. It is quite clear, however, that many members of staff in schools are only too well aware of this handy guide, to judge from their unswerving efforts to undermine the morale of their headteachers. This article reconstructs that text based on the kinds of comments I have heard in schools over the years. The trick is to make sure that the criticisms are fed back to heads so that they are only too well aware that their efforts do not just go unrewarded by any respect, but are indeed seen as clear evidence of their managerial incompetence.

There will always be enough grasses, toadies or sheer mischief-makers around to ensure that tidings of ill will are carried back to the head post haste. You do not need to search long and hard to find the obvious fall guys and girls who will be identified as the blabbermouth sources. It will be they rather than your good self who will carry the can, because they lack your devious cunning. You are the one who sows the discontent, not the one who reaps the bitter harvest to come. As far as you're concerned, Iago showed some promise in this respect, but you've learned from his mistakes. Compared to you he was an absolute beginner so there's no reason why you should come a cropper.

1. If the head consults widely on some issue and then reaches a decision which is not in your interests:
● claim that this is yet another example of the head listening to the person he or she spoke to last. "How can you know where you stand with a chameleon like this?"
● hint that there are dark reasons why Bill or Jean is the head's favourite at the moment. If Bill and Jean are both current favourites imply that the reasons are even more sinister.
● argue that the head was only consulting widely as a smokescreen because you have evidence that the decision was already taken the week before that incredibly long and boring staff meeting. "So we all sat through what was an elaborate exercise in futility. These so-called democratic staff meetings are merely a talking shop charade. I've got better things to do with my time."
● assert that this kind of so-called consensus decision is exactly the kind of weak compromise that you are bound to get with a head who is so indecisive.

2. If the head reaches a decision, which is again not in your interest, without any apparent sign of consultation:
● say that this is typical of the lack of democracy in the outfit. "Can you recall when we had any real discussion at a full staff meeting? I timed the last one and it was over in less than half an hour. They're not meetings, they're just a string of chairman's announcements. S/he might as well issue a bulletin."
● incite others to resist the drift towards tyranny by approach-

ing their unions on the issue. "The time has come to issue a challenge to government by senior management cabal. All the real decisions round here are taken in secret by the magic circle."

● encourage an artistic colleague to draw and display on the staff noticeboard a cartoon depicting the head as slave-driver with the staff as galley slaves.

● argue to others that the only way to fight despotism of this kind is to withdraw all good will and co-operation. "I guess you'll tell the head where to put the school play this year after this kick in the teeth?"

3. If the head reaches a decision which is in your favour:

● say to all your fellow 'winners' this time round that for once the head's reached the right conclusion: "it must have been more by good luck than good management." Commiserate with those who will lose out, thus demonstrating your magnanimity in victory to those who you imply have been unfairly victimised.

● suggest that this is still going to cause you difficulties: "if only the head had reached this decision last year instead of shilly-shallying around."

● later on, claim you've heard it was the governors who really came to this decision: "the head had to be dragged along kicking and screaming on this one."

4. If the head tells the staff s/he's fighting for something they want in the teeth of opposition from the governors:

● spread the word around that it's well known that the head's abrasiveness has rubbed up the governors the wrong way: "if only we had somebody at the top with an ounce of diplomacy!"

5. If the head says s/he agrees with the governors on anything which is the least bit unpopular with the staff:

● oh what you'd give for somebody at the top with a bit of backbone and some guts. "How can we ever expect to get anything from the governors with this spineless wonder in charge?" Spread the word that it's well known that the head grovels to the governors and that they despise him or her for it.

6. When the head informs the staff of promotions:

● suggest gender discrimination according to which gender is underrepresented this time round. (If an exactly equal male/ female balance is achieved you have the perfect opportunity to assert that it's "promotion by numbers these days. The head's running scared of the equal opportunities thought police.")

● suggest bias against academic subject specialists if rewards go to the pastoral care side. "You've got to be a bleeding heart around here to get a gong. This head would only be satisfied if we all taught child development and became glorified childminders. Of course if I had a poor class of degree in X, Y or Z, no doubt I'd be terrified of promoting anyone with brains."

● suggest bias against the pastoral care side if rewards go to the subject specialists. "This head is only concerned about one thing and that's exam results. I reckon it's compensation for that poor degree in X,Y or Z. All the children represent to this character is walking pound notes for the school."

● if creativity is rewarded, claim that "you've got to be two cups short of a tea set to get on in this place." If long and loyal service is rewarded argue that it's buggin's turn yet again.

7. If the head speaks about closer links with the community:

● "The parents are gods in this outfit. Don't expect any support from the head if any of them complain about you. It's the parents' word that counts every time."

● "Here we go again. Another set of evenings wasted while we act as travelling salesmen. Has this excuse for a head never heard of professional dignity?"

8. If the school rolls start to fall:

● "What can you expect when the head never leaves the office. S/he wouldn't recognise a parent if s/he fell over one."

● "This head thinks PR only stands for proportional represen- tation. We're known in this locality as the sleeping giant. Pretty soon it'll be Dozy and the seven dwarves. All our jobs will be for the chop unless s/he gets her finger out."

● "You'd think with all we've achieved in recent years, this head could at least have got us a bit of decent press coverage. I reckon s/he's frightened of reporters."

● "A bit of wining and dining the local great and the good wouldn't have done us any harm, but s/he's too puritanical to actually use a hospitality allowance. Cast your bread on the waters, I say."

9. If the head continues to maintain a teaching role:

● "What we need here is a real manager, not another part-time chalk and talk merchant. It's no wonder the organisation round here is such a shambles, we're being managed by amateurs."

10. If the head has ceased to maintain a teaching role:

● "This head's forgotten what a pupil looks like. This isn't a school any more, it's a factory. We might as well be working on the track turning out widgets. It's no wonder the organisation round here is such a shambles, we're being managed by refugees from the classroom. You've heard what they said about this clown when s/he was teaching at St. Michael's?"

11. If the head believes in management by walking around (MBWA):

● "I see the head was snooping around the classrooms again this morning while we were teaching. I wonder how s/he would react if s/he was being watched while s/he was doing whatever s/he does get up to in the Führerbunker."

12. If the head does not believe in MBWA:

● "Wouldn't it be a pleasant change if this pale imitation of Howard Hughes emerged into the light of the school day once in a blue moon, and actually saw what this job of teaching is all about? Mind you the shock of having some interest shown in my work would probably kill me."

And so on, and so on. The list of such 'damned if you do and damned if you don't' examples is potentially endless. Nor must you feel that you can only adopt one of the alternative demoralisers at a time. On almost any occasion there will be ready customers for both brands of calumny. It's just a matter of sensing which of your colleagues would prefer this or that particular variety of slander to feed their prejudices at any given time. Always remember that you are not dealing with rational, logical, fair-minded creatures but merely human beings.

IN YOUR
OWN IMAGE

f you try to do it all yourself, then this is a wooden box job", as one primary school headteacher said to me when we were discussing the increasing managerial responsibilities of heads. His vision of ending up in a coffin before reaching retirement age reminded me of another warning about managerial stress contained in that parody of Kipling's poem which goes:

> If you can fill the unforgiving minute
> With sixty seconds' worth of distance run,
> Yours is the Earth and everything that's in it,
> And a coronary before you're fifty-one.

Or, as the maxim puts it more succinctly : 'Death is nature's way of making you slow down.' If this is the government health warning that goes with the headteacher's job these days, what can be done about it? Reading articles about stress is not a good answer in my view. By the time the writers get around to suggesting ways to manage stress, they have usually depicted the possible range of symptoms in such gory detail that you feel worse than you did when you started.

There's only one real answer to job overload and that's to offload. Unfortunately this solution is easy to advance but very difficult to put into practice. The key questions are to whom do you offload and are you simply passing the stress down the line? My response to this latter point would be that if you as a headteacher have created a managerial team, then you have every right to farm out the managerial tasks. This process is not merely the absolutely indispensable act of delegation, but invaluable staff development for individuals, many of whom will be aspiring to similar positions to your own.

At this point I detect faint echoes of hollow laughter from the primary headteachers of the land as you mouth phrases such as: "Managerial team! What managerial team?" Primary headteachers appear to feel that this is a luxury reserved for their counterparts in secondary schools who are all living in executive suites surrounded by teams of non-teaching colleagues ever ready to leap into managerial action at the drop of a memo. (Pause for hollow laughter from secondary school heads.)

Not only is this vision of secondary schools a figment of your overstressed imaginations, you do indeed possess more of a managerial team potential than many of you in primary schools appear to realise. For starters, each of you has a deputy. Now I will be immediately told that in many cases this deputy has a full teaching load and is in no position to take over any of your managerial responsibilities. This is no answer. In many small primary schools the headteacher himself or herself also has a full teaching load in any case. I would agree that this is iniquitous in an age where managerial devolution from central and local government to the school has transformed the nature of the job, but in my experience these 'teaching heads' have fewer qualms about sharing out the managerial tasks amongst the 'teaching team' (which willy nilly has also to be the managerial team) however small this might be. If, on the other hand, you are in the position of either having a relatively small teaching load or none at all and your deputy has a full teaching timetable, then something is wrong with your time management.

Efforts should be made wherever possible to ensure that your deputy is in a position to share the managerial responsibilities. Far too many deputy heads become heads never having had the kinds of prior managerial experience which would enable them to take the next step up the promotional ladder with relative ease. But quite apart from these very significant benefits, there is little doubt that a two-person team is potentially better able to manage than is the one man or woman band. If we accept the findings of countless research projects on the qualities of the successful manager, then this paragon of all the virtues has to be, for example, both decisive and reflective, creative and prudent etc. In real life, very few individuals combine such disparate sets of qualities. On the other hand, it is possible for two people whose respective attributes are complementary to combine together in such a way that the whole is certainly greater than the sum of the parts.

To switch my examples for a moment from school to football management, it is in this latter sphere that many of the most famous two-person managerial 'teams' have come to prominence. To cite just one of many possible examples, there was only one significant period in my football-watching lifetime when Manchester City were winning games and trophies at a consistent rate. So much so that in my home town, the other team, the name of which escapes me for the moment, was for an all too brief period reduced to a Cinderella role. This was in the days of the highly successful Joe Mercer-Malcolm Allison partnership. For those unfamiliar with this dynamic duo, it must suffice to say that they were very different characters who worked very effectively together.

Then the late Joe Mercer left the club and the more thrusting personage of Malcolm Allison was left to manage the club single-handedly. It did not take long for those who had wondered what the more avuncular Joe had contributed to the partnership to discover that he was the essential counter-balance to Malcolm, and that without him the managerial show collapsed. Joe's worldly wisdom was shown to good effect when he was once asked why it was, if he believed himself that two person management was to be recommended, that the then manager of Leeds United, Don Revie, was so successful on his own. "You forget the role of Elsie Revie", said Joe, thus drawing attention to those many husband and wife teams which must have also been behind many a successful school.

To complete my footballing examples, at least for this article, I was at one point in my life living in another town where the local football team (in the singular this time) was managed by an ex-footballer who had in his day been a famous outside left, or left winger, as we used to call his ilk in the days when they existed on the football field as well as in politics. The first five or six signings of new players for the club which he made after his arrival were quite remarkable in that they too were all essentially left wingers, although they were called upon by him to play in a variety of other positions. This revealed what many had long suspected about this manager during his playing days, which was that he had always considered that he was capable of performing in any position on the team to better effect than anyone else. If this had been true for him, he no doubt reasoned, it must also be true for other capable left wingers. It will come as little surprise to my readers to learn that this innovative managerial policy resulted in total disaster for the club concerned.

Successful teams, then as now, needed specialists in other positions than outside left. *The results in schools of similar policies are equally disastrous.* I have seen far too many schools where the head appoints in his or her own image. A managerial team of headteacher clones is just as disastrous as a football team of left wingers. Ideally, if managerial responsibility is to be delegated, you need a team which possesses a range of skills, so that the individual task can be allocated to the most appropriate set of hands.

Furthermore, the logic of my argument leads, I hope, to the conclusion that for an efficient headteacher, any appointment to the teaching staff is potentially, if not actually, an appointment to the managerial team. There are now far too many managerial responsibilities in any school for the staff as a whole not to have a share in carrying them out. All members of a school staff are managers, even if some are more managerial than others. As I have tried to argue, the real trick as a headteacher is to have on your managerial team, staff who will complement your many undoubted qualities rather than simply reproduce them.

The best way I know to go about this is first of all for you yourself to complete the self analysis inventory in Dr. Meredith Belbin's book *Management Teams - Why They Succeed or Fail* which was published by Heinemann in 1985. This should give you some very clear indications of your own strengths and weaknesses as a member of a management team. I know of few other instruments so tried and tested by both practitioners and fellow researchers, and so universally praised as a means of identifying the roles to which management team members are best suited. The next step is to get your management team colleagues to go through the same process. You then need to sit down together and identify any obvious 'gaps' in the management team as it is presently constituted. Remember, however, that in smaller teams one person can play more than one role as long as they display some strength in that area.

Secondly, if one or more of the team move on, you should be alert to the possibility of making a new appointment who would bring those compensatory strengths to the team. This is certainly an interesting variant on the usual list of criteria that are drawn up as person specifications on such occasions.

Thirdly you might consider doing a trawl of the budding managers on the staff to see if any individual already possesses the particular talents you need to complete the team and to consider drafting that individual in on occasions where it would be worthwhile. This is most useful in my experience when the missing link in the management chain is the ideas person who Belbin argues may need to be 'planted' into the team to provide the creative spark on the key occasions when it is required.

DELEGATION AS ABDICATION:

OR HOW NOT TO HAND WORK OVER.

1.0 Setting the scene.

1.1 Don't have a management team: have a strict hierarchy in which everyone knows his or her place in the pecking order. That makes it so much easier to know who should be delegating to whom.

1.2 Don't try to communicate to your subordinates any vision of where you think the outfit is heading. You probably haven't got a vision anyway. Most of the time it feels like steering the ship from the bridge with no radar and in a dense fog. All you know is that there are icebergs out there somewhere.

1.3 Don't bother setting personal standards. You're the boss and you've earned the right to take the odd afternoon off. You need your rest and relaxation. It's important that your subordinates realise the stresses and strains of your job mean you need more time off than they do.

1.4 Make it clear that you could do any of the jobs which need to be done better than your subordinates.....if you had the time and the inclination.

1.5 Don't plan ahead to anticipate the need for delegation. Delegation is what you do when there's a crisis, and you define what a crisis is. Crisis management is management.

2.0 When to delegate

2.1 When there are too many tasks piled up on your desk to allow you to fit in that foursome on Wednesday afternoon. (This is one of your definitions of a crisis.)

2.2 When there are too many boring routine chores you can't be bothered to deal with yourself. (You didn't get where you are today by doing boring routine chores.)

2.3 When there are some parts of tasks you fancy less than others. Hang on to the parts you like and farm out the rest.

2.4 When you've got some task to complete which is so complex that you don't even begin to understand how to tackle it. (An air of studied nonchalance is called for when you hand this kind of job over. You need to give the impression that you could have done this one before breakfast if you'd bothered to get up in time. After that opening they'd rather die than admit they couldn't fathom it out.)

3.0 Finding someone to delegate the job to

3.1 Go along to the dining room and see who's free.

3.2 Pass it on to one of your deputies. If they can't do it, they can always pass it down the line. That's what hierarchies are for.

3.3 Don't waste your time thinking out who might be best able to do the job, or who might benefit from the experience. Whoever said that delegation should be a form of staff development was just a good confidence trickster. The whole point of delegation is to get the job off your back.

4.0 How to delegate

4.1 Say what the job is and tell Jill or Fred to get on with it. Make certain they realise it's your job not theirs, but unfortunately they'll have to do it for you because you haven't the time.

4.2 You haven't time either for lengthy consultations or brief-ings. After all you wouldn't be delegating if there wasn't a crisis. For the same reason it doesn't matter a jot what their current workloads are. They'll just have to drop those while they get on with your task in hand. But woe betide them if they use this as an excuse for not producing the monthly returns on time.

4.3 Don't bother setting a deadline: it's quite clear enough that you want the job done as quickly as possible. If Jill has the nerve to ask when you want it done, say by yesterday!

4.4 Don't check whether the task has been understood: if you haven't used the "I could have done this before breakfast" ploy then Fred will soon be back snivelling if he hasn't grasped it first time round. That's just par for the course. They never seem to have the necessary self-confidence to take real decisions themselves anyway. As for risk-taking on their part, that'll be the day!

4.5 Make it clear they're on their own from now on in and can't expect back-up support. Your secretary is already far too busy. Offer them every assistance short of actual help. As soon as it leaves your desk as far as you're concerned it's SEP (Someone Else's Problem).

4.6 Don't inform anyone else that you have delegated this or that task to Fred or Jill. Time enough for that when the job's done. If it's done well then you can grab the credit. If it's done badly, you can inform your superiors that your subordinates have let you down again.

4.7 Don't bother specifying in advance what outcomes or results you are hoping for. If you had a clue you probably wouldn't have delegated in the first place! The jobs you're clear about you do yourself anyway (most times).

4.8 From time to time say to your secretary that if you want a job done well you'd better do it yourself. You can be sure the message about what you think of the quality of your subordinates' performance will be all round the building in no time.

4.9 Don't use the episode as a learning exercise for all concerned. If you had time for developmental de-briefings once the tasks were completed you wouldn't need to delegate! It's all well and good those ivory tower theorists writing about the need for constructive feedback. They're not living in the real world! You've never met a writer on management yet who in your opinion could organise the proverbial in a brewery.

UPWARD DELEGATION

An official farewell dinner to the headteacher of a school in the north of England took place recently. This school was one of those with a particular church connection and the head was of the right reverend tendency. In his own speech he looked back on his many years in the school during which time it had grown from what he described as its humble ecclesiastical origins to an institution three times the size, with a high reputation to match. "I have always seen myself as Peter the Builder", he proclaimed with suitably religious overtones.

His deputy of long standing had to follow this peroration and he began in the following vein: "As you have all heard, the headmaster has always seen himself as Peter the Builder. I have also always seen him as Peter the Builder. And I have always seen myself as Chris the chap who picked up the bricks that Peter the

Builder dropped!" All those who knew the two of them realised the truth of that statement.

"Peter the Builder" had only been able to engineer the school's growth because of a personality that could hardly be described as underbearing. In the process there had been not only a lot of bricks dropped, but many feathers which had been ruffled. Chris was the ideal deputy in these circumstances because he smoothed ruffled feathers and applied ointment to toes on which bricks had sometimes fallen from a great height. Between them Peter and Chris had been a great double act.

This particular style of double act has been used to similar good effect in many schools with headteachers who would score very highly on what we call in management jargon 'task considera-tion', and with deputies who are very much more concerned with 'people consideration'. (Which is not to say that I have not observed cases of role reversal, where the head expects the deputy to play the task-oriented role.) In most organisations you want to make sure that the job is properly executed before the deadline expires, but at the same time you want to preserve good working relationships for future as well as present group harmony. Unfortunately the two considerations are not always compatible with each other.

Any one manager trying to do both things at once may either seem to be hypocritical or suffering from split personality. It is so much easier for one manager to be the task specialist and another to be the human face of management. Such a separa-tion of management functions is apparently not unknown in a partnership of police detectives working on a case together, at least if this recurring theme in countless TV serials is anything to go by. But most secondary schools of any significant size these days have more than one deputy headteacher and here we move on from the partnership of two people to the larger managerial teams. As I intimated in an earlier chapter on this theme (*In Your Own Image*), it is, in any case, my view that all teachers are managers and the more that headteachers see all their staff as part of the school's managerial team the more successful the school is likely to be.

Viewed from this perspective, any school has a managerial team which consists of the whole staff, including non-teaching staff. You only have to consider for a moment the key managerial role of the caretaker, for example, to realise the validity of this statement. All staff in schools are responsible for the management of other people because in the final analysis it is the management of the pupils, and the management of their learning in particular, that is the *raison d'être* of the staff. The main problem, however, facing any head who wants to develop staff in their various managerial roles and capacities is that some of them will not accept without a struggle the notion that they also have managerial responsibilities. These members of staff will hold firm to the view that management is what the head and the deputies are paid to do. What is more, even those who do accept the idea that all staff are managers in some respects will have probably become very skilled over the years in the black art of upward delegation.

The management textbooks that define delegation as "the act of getting tasks accomplished by empowering a subordinate in the organisational hierarchy to carry out the job" have only told one part of the story. In my experience that's by no means the full reality of delegation in everyday organisational life. It is equally true that subordinates can be past masters at delegating to those higher up the hierarchy than themselves.

The main perpetrators are not going to own up to the practice and their victims higher up the hierarchy are usually unaware of what is happening to them or they wouldn't let the practice continue. All that such bosses are aware of is a vague realisation that their crushing workload never seems to diminish. When they try to do something about this by delegating, they discover that they end up having more on their plate than they had before they decided to delegate in the first place. This is the kind of boss who is frequently heard to be saying such things as: "Oh, give it to me. It's quicker to do it yourself." If it is indeed always quicker, and less bother, to do it yourself, then your time management skills need considerable sharpening. You certainly need to be alert to the characteristic tricks of upward delegation.

The first of these is the 'chance meeting' (usually outside the office or the normal arena where management activities are officially deemed to take place) when your subordinate says in passing, and apparently off-the-cuff: "Oh, by the way, were you aware that suchabody is up to no good over the something or other affair? I think it needs taking in hand before it gets any worse." If you then mutter something like: "Ok I'll look into it", your fate is sealed. The buck has been neatly passed up the line. If you forget to look into it because you then meet three other people in the corridor who also pass on their problems of the day to you, then you have effectively been booby trapped. When the explosion occurs, as it surely will, two or three months hence, your subordinate will be very quick to remind you, or quite possibly your superior, that he or she had drawn your attention to the dangers some considerable time ago. Not only can the subordinate not accept any responsibility for picking up the pieces (that's now another job for you), but there is the unspoken message that this is just another example of your general managerial ineptitude.

So what should you have done? Well the first move in the usually recommended Sicilian defence in this game of managerial chess is to respond to the 'chance remark' along the following lines. "That's very interesting. Would you please put that down in writing for me for tomorrow." This puts the onus back onto the subordinate. Putting something in writing is often the last thing he or she wants to do in such circumstances. More likely than not, there will be a head stuck round the door tomorrow morning and a cheery comment to the effect that the suchabody affair is all cleared up now. "Something of a storm in a teacup." Don't be taken in by this. Say you're delighted to hear it but you'd still like a note about the matter "just for the record". If the note fails to convince you that the storm is likely to stay confined to the teacup, ask your subordinate to suggest a plan of action. Subordinates in this situation are not only hoist with their own petard, they are far less likely to leave any more petards lying around your office in future. Next time they may even take prompt action in the early stages to ensure that the flash bang stage is never reached.

Another well known ploy in this particular game is the scrawled memo which conveys something like the following message. "As the chairman of the School Learning Resources Committee I was asked at our meeting last night to clarify a number of issues with you. What is going to be the future learning resources policy in this organisation now that such and such an event has occurred or is likely to occur?" and so on and so on. On no account answer such questions. Much better to respond as follows: "Thank you for your undated memo on the subject of learning resources which I received on the 23rd of May. I am very pleased to see that your committee has so promptly recognised that such and such an event has important potential consequences for our future learning resources policy. I would, therefore, be gratified if your committee would now draft some constructive proposals as to what our future policy ought to be, were these circumstances to arise. As you will recall, I established your committee for the express purpose of offering advice in precisely this area, and I now look forward to receiving your recommendations on the matter by Friday 2 June. They will then be discussed at the meeting of the Senior Management Team to be held on Wednesday 7 June."

After a prolonged campaign of this kind your subordinates will begin to get the message that bringing you their managerial problems will not ensure that they spend the week-end sailing while you wrestle with these problems on their behalf. On the contrary, you should demonstrate that bringing their problems to you may mean they will never see the sea-side again.

This is not, of course, to say that there won't be times when staff have to bring problems to you which they are genuinely incapable of handling at their level. One of the acid tests of their future managerial potential is their ability to spot which problems fall into this category and their ability to present them to you in a readily comprehensible form. What it boils down to in the end is whether your subordinates are under your control as opposed to you being under their control. The trouble is that there are too many managers in education who get considerable satisfaction in taking over their subordinates' problems. It gives them a sense of well-being because they can convince themselves that they are not only needed but indispensable. I have a message for such managers. Nobody in the managerial world is indispensable, although I do have to admit that some are more dispensable than others!

HEADSPEAK

Over recent years I have come to the conclusion that there might well be a need for a glossary of headteacher terminology that would allow parents, teachers and governors etc to make more sense of the phrases that trip off the forked tongues of Machiavellian headteachers. So for starters I present the following:

Our examination results last year were second to none in the area.
I know we came appallingly low in the league tables but there is still that dreadful outfit down the road which did even worse.

The day of the dictatorial head has gone. We operate as a Senior Management Team (SMT).
If anything goes badly wrong I need scapegoats on to whom I can pass the blame.

In this school the pupils come first.
Given the state of our budget, losing pupils is a financial disaster whereas losing staff is a definite financial plus.

We are at present re-evaluating our skills mix.
That's a little bit of current management jargon to dazzle you. What it ultimately will mean when you've got the glare out of your eyes is three classics staff out and two computer whiz kids in.

We are currently monitoring the school policy on bullying.
In response to your awkward question, I have to admit to myself at least that there have been three very nasty incidents of physical victimisation recently which I am determined to keep out of the local press at all costs.

We fully intend to take appropriate action in the unlikely event of a less than favourable report from our working party.
With any luck this will all blow over if I can delay the report for long enough, but I might be forced to take avoiding action if it does go public.

We are keeping a very careful eye on the developing situation.
This is the first I've heard of it, and somebody's going to swing on the yard-arm for not keeping me informed about this one.

I'm glad you asked me that question.
For once the early warning system has worked, matey, so this is one of your time-bombs that we've already defused.

That's a very interesting question, but I think I'll need to give you a bit of background before I can respond sensibly to it.
I desperately need to stall on this until I can clear my wits enough to come up with something that doesn't sound like nonsense on stilts.

We can hardly go back now on a policy which was only decided upon after the widest possible consultation.
I know that dodgy deal on the new computer system is blowing up in my face, but if I go down I'm going to take most of the governing body with me.

Thank you, Mr Jones, you know that I have always welcomed constructive criticism in staff meetings.

Flattery and praise wrapped up as comment are always welcome William old boy.

I'm sure you will all agree that the display of pupils' essays in the foyer demonstrates that our traditional standards have been maintained.

They damn well ought to be good. We made the little treasures rewrite them four times.

I have asked my Senior Deputy to look into this one and to prepare a report.

This looks like a no-win situation to me and the further I distance myself from it the better. Jim's only a year to go to retirement. Could you suggest a more appropriate fall guy?

This is a personal and private matter which I am not prepared to discuss.

My salary is an issue only for the governing body and myself. It would only demoralise the rest of the staff if they knew the personal financial package I've managed to negotiate through the governors. Even I think it's almost obscene! Three cheers for the Local Management of Schools!

I am sure you all appreciate the much more up-market image which our school publicity literature is now projecting on our behalf. We will all be the beneficiaries.

Some more than others! Mind you, that marketing consultancy has cost us a packet. Still, "selling ourselves" sounds so much better than "lying" or even "being economical with the actuality".

It's my great pleasure to welcome Ms Johnson to her first meeting of the Senior Management Team. I am sure we all agree that the female viewpoint at this level in the school needs some reinforcement.

Over my dead body it does. Still this should be an effective pre-emptive strike against any attempt by Ms Bradshaw to take us to the Equal Opps. Thought Police.

So that's the view of the Senior Management Team which has

been reached after lengthy discussion on this issue. **I would now welcome constructive suggestions for improvements to this policy before we go public on it. Please could I have these in writing by this Friday afternoon at the latest.**

I have already decided what we are going to do about this. Having steamrollered my views through the SMT, I am now going to implicate the rest of you through this phoney consultation exercise.

It serves no purpose whatsoever to squabble amongst ourselves when faced with this external threat.

The sooner some people realise that we're all in the same boat the better. We all need to pull together at times like these. Nothing shuts down internal criticism like the notion of the common enemy at the gates. We may be all in the same boat on this one but I'm not travelling steerage and my private lifeboat is already fully laden with provisions. Meanwhile back on board the Titanic.....

I hear what you say.

I have not the slightest intention of doing anything whatsoever about this whinge. Just keep on taking the tablets.

School uniform is obligatory in this school because it prevents ostentatious displays of wealth through clothes and fashion.

School uniform is obligatory in this school because that's the sort of thing parents look for when choosing where to send their offspring. And what the punters want....

School performance league tables are full of errors; they are socially divisive; they are an open invitation to some schools to massage their results...

...up until the point when this school gets some reasonably good results and then they are a true and fair reflection of the school's achievement.

Appraisal in this school is all about staff development and personal and professional growth at the individual level.

Appraisal in this school is a very useful means of (a) underlining who is accountable to whom, and (b) achieving organisational targets. The system is more important than the individual.

This will be a challenging opportunity for you.
This is a back-breaking and/or mind-numbing chore that I can find nobody else to take on.

I know you're the kind of person who's always looking for a challenge.
The only challenge you've ever looked for is how to draw a salary without actually working.

This new responsibility might well stand you in good stead in your future career.
On the other hand, it might well not make the slightest difference one way or the other.

You play ball with us on this one, and we'll see what we can do for you.
You play ball with us on this one.

I would like to think that our drama section could be seen by the outside world as a centre of excellence in this school.
It's about time you stopped running those bog-standard productions of *The Merchant of Venice* and the like. If you want promotion, you'd better come up with something a touch more spectacular. How about *The Sound of Music* on roller skates? That should be worth a good few column inches in the press.

If you carry out this task to our satisfaction, I promise that you will not be forgotten if and when promotion possibilities occur.
This is not only not a written guarantee, it's not even worth the paper it's not printed on. (If Sam Goldwyn could bend 'em, why can't I bend his immortal words?)

We have that matter under very active consideration.
I might get around to having a look at this one sometime soon if the pressure continues to mount.

It would be entirely improper for me to comment on a speculative press report on such a delicate issue at this time.
Great! My leak to the local rag about the possible closure of old Fred's excuse for a school is working already.

THE HEAD RULES *OK*

1. The head is right.
2. The head is always right.
3. Even if a member of staff is right, rule 1 still applies.
4. If a member of staff has a good idea, that becomes the head's idea.
5. The head doesn't eat or drink, s/he takes light refreshment.
6. The head doesn't nod off in the office, s/he is occupied.
7. The head is never late, s/he is detained.
8. The head never leaves the building, s/he is called elsewhere.
9. The head never reads the newspaper, s/he scans the environment.
10. The head never brags, s/he publicises the school's successes.
11. The head does not whinge, s/he voices legitimate concerns.
12. The head does not make financial cuts, s/he makes budgetary adjustments.
13. The head does not sack staff, s/he lets individuals go and downsizes the school establishment.

14. The head never forgets anything, it is under consideration.
15. The head never loses anything, it is under active consideration.
16. The head never spreads gossip, s/he circulates reports from reliable sources.
17. The head does not encourage grassing, s/he relies on informed sources.
18. The head never passes the buck, s/he delegates.
19. The head never blocks staff communication with outsiders, s/he takes care of boundary management.
20. The head can accept constructive criticism, s/he can not accept disloyalty. (The head defines when criticism is destructive and/or disloyal.)
21. The head does not have cronies, s/he has senior colleagues.
22. The head did not wish to become a freemason. Forging links with the community is an onerous and essential part of the head's job.
23. The head does not enjoy playing golf. S/he is cultivating influential stakeholders.
24. The head does not take a disproportionate pay increase, s/he is awarded an appropriate incentive bonus by the governing body. This bonus is reluctantly accepted by the head as the inevitable consequence of market forces.
25. The head does not dictate, s/he promulgates the outcomes of lengthy consultations.
26. The head does not spend an excessive amount of money on the furnishings and trappings of the head's office, s/he creates a suitable ambience for visitors.
27. The head does not spend capitation on drink, s/he has a hospitality/entertainment budget.
28. The head does not take the most unpleasant decisions, s/he informs the staff of the outcomes of the governing body's deliberations.
29. The head is never on holiday, s/he is at a conference.
30. The school does not have a secretary, the head has.

THE ART OF NON-COMMUNICATION

A GUIDE FOR HEADTEACHERS WHO WISH TO COVER THEIR TRACKS

One cynical captain of industry of my acquaintance reckons that the true art of communication for any manager who wishes to survive is best summed up by Talleyrand's dictum that speech was given to man to hide his thoughts. This latter quotation may now be seen as couched in somewhat sexist and, therefore, politically incorrect terms, but coming from someone who survived one Napoleon Bonaparte, two French revolutions, and innumerable accusations of corruption, treason and the like, it is well worth thinking about. Indeed I would argue that Talleyrand probably didn't go far enough with this maxim, as far as some heads are concerned.

If speech is best used to disguise one's true managerial intentions, then this is even more the case with anything which these heads are forced to put into writing. The kind of heads I have in mind only resort to the word processor for communication when all else has failed, or they are acting under extreme duress. They work on the principle that memos should not be written to convey information but to cover their backs if anyone ever finds the bodies. If memos etc. are dictated and signed by their secretaries on their behalf, they can always claim later that the wording was wrongly transcribed in any case. The problem is that the DFE is increasingly laying down the law these days about the official papers they have to issue under their own signature, so the production of some documents is unfortunately becoming unavoidable. Let's take a couple of examples from my new manual for such heads to demonstrate that this need not necessarily be the calamity they fear.

1. The Staff Handbook
The key point to bear in mind about the staff handbook is that nobody ever reads it. So it doesn't really matter if you last revised it in 1978 as long as the cover has the current year inscribed upon it. Even the insomniacs on the staff would not regard it as bedtime reading matter. One headteacher has actually conducted a systematic research study into this phenomenon with her own staff handbook over the last three years and I am now able to report her conclusive evidence that no-one ever reads it.

Her research methodology can be quickly summarised as follows: whenever any members of staff over the last three years have buttonholed her when she has occasionally been caught out of her bunker, (taking the odd promenade around the school, by the way, is now known in the trade as MBWA or Management By Waltzing Around), her response has invariably been that they would probably find that the answer to the question they posed was on page 16 of the staff handbook.

The answer served a number of purposes. First of all, from the winces of pain on the face of her interlocutors, it was clearly, and quite correctly, taken as a rebuke to anyone foolish enough to try to elicit responses from her while she was on the move which could later be used in evidence against her during court proceedings. (Those, by the way, who consider that word of mouth communication, either face to face or on the phone, is ephemeral, and, therefore, later deniable, are not up to date with modern technology as the briefest of glances at the tabloid coverage of the "newsworthy" men and women of our day will demonstrate.)

Secondly it has given her an entirely spurious reputation as a walking staff handbook encyclopaedia, the bureaucratic equivalent of the Wisden cricket buff.

Thirdly it has confirmed her original research hypothesis that nobody, herself included, actually reads the handbook even when specifically referred to it. She is prepared to accept that she might have hit lucky once in a hundred times, but that must still leave 99 cases where page 16 contained nothing remotely connected to the point at issue. The aficionados of this particular sport will already have spotted that the use of the word "probably" gave her the perfect come-back if anyone had ever returned thumbing page 16 thoughtfully. BUT NO-ONE EVER HAS.

Indeed, an even cruder research methodology of issuing the handbook wrapped in cling film has also trapped many an unsuspecting staff member. At some point in the school year she has swooped on an individual and asked him or her just to look up a particular point in the staff handbook for her. Some individuals are crafty enough to claim to have temporarily mislaid it but she reckons you'd be surprised how many make a reflex grab for it only to reveal it as just as perfectly gift wrapped as the day it was issued. I note that the NCC and SEAC have been using a similar strategy for their publications in conjunction with inspectorates; so be warned. In their new merged state these quangos are most unlikely to discard their former devious practices.

Remove the cling film from your copy of the non-statutory guidance on Tibetan Handloom Weaving immediately it arrives, bung it into the ringbinder and only then put it on your bookshelf to gather dust with all the others. (You don't need to grapple with the tortuous complexities of it all. You've far too much administration to be involved in teaching and you've delegated curriculum anyway.) Chances are, however, that it will be out of date by the time the newly privatised inspectorate swoop down on you, because some right wing think tank will have decided that there were still distinct residual traces of the devil's hoofmark of progressivism. If you are then caught in possession of an earlier copy which still contains sections on the footloom heresy, take a tip from those in earlier periods of the Inquisition who were not clamouring to be martyrs, and claim that it was only being retained as archive material to remind you how far and how fast standards in education have improved in recent years.

There will be others who claim to have incontrovertible evidence that there are members of staff who do read the handbook because their Heads of English Departments have dropped them a line soon after publication to point out that an infinitive has been split on page 23. (Such a memo is usually couched in jocular tones but don't be deceived by this. As far as the Head of English is concerned you have not only committed a mortal sin but once again demonstrated that he or she would be an infinitely superior manager of the school's affairs.) This only goes to prove my point, however. If the Head of English had actually read page 23, he or she would have been bound to notice that your description of the work of the Schools Council was now a trifle passé. All he or she has in fact done is to unwrap the handbook and then pick a page at random where the inevitable error has not taken long to find. This is not a sign of scholarship, erudition and conscientiousness, but a pathetic attempt to pull the wool over your eyes which only manifests a nitpicking inability to see the wood for the trees.

2. The School Prospectus

The difficulty here is that some people do actually read this document. That's the bad news. The good news is that these people are the parents (existing, or more likely, potential) of the pupils in your school, and not the pupils themselves. The pupils, if they ever did read anything as boring as a school prospectus, would immediately spot the gap between the rhetoric and the reality, but in the case of parents you can follow the estate agent's adage that you can fool an awful lot of the people an awful lot of the time. Only recently, it seems, have people rumbled the true meanings of terms such as 'suitable for modernisation' or 'in a lively neighbourhood', etc. I think, however, that there is still considerable scope for creative writing when it comes to the school prospectus. I offer, therefore, some possible alternative renderings of descriptions that might not quite suggest the ambience you wish to convey to the potential punters in your area.

Rhetoric: This has traditionally been a community based school which has encouraged parental support of out of school activities. We are now keen that children from the more outlying districts should be able to derive the benefits of our innovative curriculum.

Reality: The immediate catchment area of the school contains the most notorious thieves' kitchen in the region.

Rhetoric: The school's foundation dates back to a charitable trust of the sixteenth century. We believe in the tried and trusted values of continuity and stability in an ever changing world.

Reality: The school buildings should have been demolished before the Second World War but this was postponed in case the Luftwaffe did the job for free. After the war the site to which you should have moved was used to house a cinema which was later transformed into a bingo hall and has now become a supermarket. (Thereby demonstrating the priority generally afforded to education in England. The Germans have now realised that they can, therefore, triumph over us in Europe without having to waste valuable Deutschemarks on aerial bombardment.)

Rhetoric: In recent years no other school in the area has improved its record of examination successes to such an extent. The school's motto of *mens sana in corpore sano* aptly embodies our philosophy of turning out the rounded individual who will be well equipped to compete in life's unending struggle for excellence.

Reality: You have only managed to jack up the previously deplorable exam results by a ruthless policy of teaching to the test and cramming for the examinations to the exclusion of anything else.

Rhetoric: Durnstone Comprehensive is the most recently constructed school in the borough and won the prestigious

Allcock Architectural Award for School Design in 1966. The open plan aspects of this purpose-built comprehensive school have enabled us to accommodate more pupils on the premises than were originally envisaged, but the school is still oversubscribed. A modern school for a modern environment.

Reality: Your school is basically a typical example of 1960s self-destruct. The flat roof has been an irreparable disaster. The distinctive open corridor arcades, by which the architect hoped to give a Florentine appearance to the exterior, have only served to expose the pupils to the risk of frost bite in the bitterly cold north east winds (and that's in June and July). Your only advantage is that the other secondary schools in the borough are housed in Victorian buildings and their exteriors have not been enhanced by the industrial pollutants of the last century.

Rhetoric: This newly confirmed Grant Maintained School confidently expects to build on its reputation as a friendly intimate establishment, where the head knows every pupil by name, by seeking to enrol only those pupils whose parents are keen for them to succeed. Interviews for parents will be held during the next term and forms can be obtained from the School Registrar at the above address. A new school for a new era.

Reality: Your grimy Victorian school was due to be closed in the LEA's development plan due to plummeting rolls. You managed to panic enough of the remaining parents to petition for opting out and the DFE has just granted you Grant Maintained status. Your initial grant will amply cover the cost of sand blasting the exterior.

Conclusion: If you think this suspicion of rhetoric is only a sign of our corrupt times then please look again at the writings about our old friend Talleyrand. At an elaborate Paris reception he once attended, the names of the official guests were being publicly announced on arrival by the liveried footman. Then came an announcement from the host himself that the Italian ambassador would unfortunately not be present as he had suffered a heart attack en route and had died on his way to the hospital. Quick as a flash, Talleyrand turned to one of his entourage and said: "I wonder what the real reason is?"

THE HEAD'S GUIDE TO REPORT WRITING

When I recently conducted some research into headteacher-governing body relationships, I rapidly became aware of the crucial importance of the heads' reports to their governing bodies.This was the main means of formal communication from the one to the other. It was all the more surprising, then, that there appeared to be no guidelines issued by the LEAs which I surveyed as to how heads might structure such reports.

The documents I saw varied enormously in both quantity and, in my view, quality. There was, however, one recurrent leitmotif in many of the reports I studied and this was the heads' attempt to demonstrate to their governors that despite all the problems faced by the school, each term had been yet another triumph against all the odds.

Bearing this fundamental message in mind I have attempted to create a specimen headteacher's report that should serve as a model for all heads across the country.

1. Buildings, Fabric and Maintenance

1.1 The severe gales in March caused considerable damage to the section of roof over the main hall. The temporary repairs do appear to have improved the acoustics however. The LEA has assured us that permanent repairs will figure in their "rolling programme" along with the other items featured in my reports in recent years.

1.2 The Friends of Dimchurch School have kindly donated an extra vacuum cleaner. This means that the three members of the cleaning staff now have two vacuum cleaners between them and we confidently expect the standard of school cleaning to improve depite the further cuts in their hours. It will be recalled that the LEA's earlier experiment with contract cleaning had to be discontinued after the visit of the Environmental Health Officer in connection with rodent infestation. Governors will be pleased to learn that there have been only two 'sightings' this term.

1.3 The Fire Brigade conducted a spot inspection in February. The officers were impressed at the speed with which the pupils were able to vacate the school. I was able to point out that they had nightly practice in these procedures and that it was rare to find a pupil still on the premises by 16.02 hours most evenings. Even so, the school staff usually managed to show an even more impressive turn of speed on most occasions.

1.4 The discontinuance of all school clubs due to the "industrial dispute" has had the advantage that the school premises can be hired in their entirety by local community groups from the afternoon onwards. There have been some interesting and profitable lettings since this function was delegated to us by the LEA as part of the first stage in the programme of Local Management of Schools (LMS). I understand that some parents have expressed some disquiet at the nature of some of the groups which have hired the premises, but I can assure you that 'The Knights of the Iron Cross (Siegfried Division)' have been one of the most orderly and tidy clubs to use our school in recent years. They have certainly been a considerable improvement on the local church youth club in this respect.

1.5 The five year plan to complete the internal decoration of the school should be completed next term. I would like to pay tribute to all those parents who have given so generously of their time and effort in this aspect of the self-help programme. I should also like to thank the LEA for its generous donation of emulsion paint. It is a pity that the LEA's finances do not run to gloss paint, and if any local industrialist would care to make a contribution in this respect it would be most gratefully received. Potential donors may care to bear in mind the school's policy of naming annual prizes after our benefactors.

1.6 The breakdown of the school heating system caused us to reintroduce the intensive physical activities programme. This has served us well in the past and once again we found that if staff and pupils did not remain static for more than a minute at a time there was little danger of frostbite. We also expect this programme to pay rich dividends at the annual schools' sports competition.

1.7 Later that month we had the small fire under the school stage which was so unfortunately reported in the local media. In fact the so-called "conflagration" was quickly contained and the stage is still usable in part. Although the boys concerned claimed that they had lit the fire during the lunch hour in order to keep warm, it is strongly suspected that surreptitious smoking was the real cause. The reduction in timetabled provision for health education due to the exigencies of the National Curriculum may have been a contributory factor here. (Please see the later section on curriculum).

1.8 The discovery of the asbestos lagging in the ceiling over the refectory has once again demonstrated the value of the twice-yearly safety audit. We have been assured by the LEA officers responsible that unless pupils stamp heavily on the floor of the room above the dining room there is little danger of asbestos fibres escaping into the atmosphere, and the necessary repairs have been added to their rolling programme along with the others referred to above.

1.9 The school library has benefitted considerably from the jumble sale organised by the pupils themselves. Not only was the magnificent sum of £52.13 raised from the proceeds, but as so few of the books which were donated were actually bought, they have been transferred to the library thus increasing our basic book stock by some 300%. The titles might not have been in every case those we would have chosen to purchase, but we have long since learned not to look gift horses in the mouth.

1.10 I should like to end this section of the report by paying tribute to the work of the school caretaker, Mr Johnson, or 'Godfather' as he is affectionately known to the pupils. Despite his recurrent back problems he has never failed to be on hand to open and close the school premises for the various community groups which have hired the school. He has also not allowed the overtime payments he has acquired as a result of these services to make him overlook the fact that his first loyalty is to the school and its pupils. It has been very gratifying to see the way he has organised the work schemes for pupils which have given them valuable experience of the industrial conditions they can expect to encounter in the local factories later in their lives. I am sure that there is no truth whatsoever in the rumour that it was sabotage by the stoking gang which put the boilers out of action in January.

2.0 Staffing

I began the last report by warning governors that the school's falling rolls might cause severe staffing problems for us this year. In the event the sudden departure of Mrs Winkley, Miss Jones and Mr Watson at the end of the Summer term meant that we were able to reduce our teaching staff to two teachers below our new allocation by a process of 'natural wastage'. Mr Watson obtained a post with Securicor,

Mrs Winkley has joined Her Majesty's prison service and Mr Jones is now specialising in fire insurance. I am sure that their experience over the years at Dimchurch will stand them in good stead in their new careers where they all assure me they will be earning considerably more than they were with us.

2.1 We were still left with the awkward decision of how to decide which of our existing deputy heads should take up the one continuing post to which we are now justified. However, the unfortunate accident to Mrs Jenkins resolved the issue in a way which none of us would have wished. As we are awaiting the report of the Health and Safety Inspectorate and the case is still sub judice I will make no further comment at this point in time.

2.2 The combined effect of these events was such that we had three vacancies to fill for the start of the school year. It was disappointing that we had so few suitable applicants for the posts in question. In the end it was only due to the LEA's 'European Trawl' that we were able to fill the vacancies at all. We were, therefore, delighted to welcome Ms van der Dussen, Mr Busch, and Mr Beernaert in September. It was a pity that Mr Busch felt that he had to return to Germany so soon after joining us but our other new colleagues appear to have settled in well despite some initial teething troubles. The pupils seem to have few communication problems with the new staff now and we have all learned to appreciate that our membership of the European Union can bring unexpected benefits.

2.3 Our other staffing problem at the start of the school year concerned the three school cleaners who declined to stay on under the terms offered by 'Cleaning Up', the private firm to which the LEA has now sub-contracted school cleaning in this area. We were sorry to lose our existing cleaning staff who had given loyal service to the school, and we marked their departure with a suitable leaving ceremony. The new company appears to employ an interestingly varied workforce since we are never sure from one day to the next who will turn up. Although the individuals concerned may change from day to day, there is a uniformly brisk approach to their duties: the job is now completed in about half the time previously expended. There are now rumours circulating to the effect that the Chairman of the Education Committee, who has recently returned from a fact-finding mission to Japan, is of the view that it would be sound training in citizenship for the pupils to clean the school themselves.

2.4 Governors will recall that they insisted at the end of last term that the school should take back Wayne Clapham who had been excluded on account of the unseemly fracas with Ms Johnson. I have to report that Ms Johnson's refusal to take him back into her class was supported by her trade union. There was a general reluctance on the part of other teachers, who have witnessed what they regard as Wayne's anti-social tendencies over recent years, to take over the responsibility for this particular pupil. I consequently placed Wayne with Mr Busch, and then, following the latter's sudden departure for Germany, with Ms van der Dussen. I regret to have to inform you that I have now felt obliged to exclude Wayne yet again. It is not possible to offer conclusive evidence that it was Wayne who wrote the offending text on Ms van der Dussen's blackboard, but it does seem very plausible that he was the author of the phrase: "I got the first Kraut and now I'll get you." I, therefore, feel I had no alternative and I seek the governors' advice and support. Ms van der Dussen is especially upset at the fact that some pupils appear to make no distinction between the Germans and the Dutch and this has led to the happy outcome that we are planning a 'European Week' for the end of term which should help to raise pupils' awareness in this area.

2.5 As far as staff development is concerned, Mr Meakin is still pursuing his advanced Diploma in the Martial Arts and Mr Combey is taking a course in Dutch for Beginners at our local FE College. Ms van der Dussen has kindly offered to help him with extra conversation lessons and she has also agreed to plan a school trip to Amsterdam with him later this year. I understand that this is a charming old city with a rich historic tradition and I am sure that parents will be keen for their children to go on this trip. There should be none of the problems that we encountered with our Winter trip to the Austrian mountains last year when the lack of snow was a direct cause of the boredom which led to excess energy being so lamentably misdirected in certain cases.

2.6 For our in-house staff training we had two of our LEA advisers visit the school on October 19th. for a workshop on the place of education for economic and industrial under-standing in the National Curriculum. Their interesting workshop design involved an initial 'ice-breaking' exercise which demonstrably removed any staff inhibitions. This was followed by a 'snowball' where individuals were encouraged to write down ideas, share them with a fellow member of staff and then report back to the whole school staff in plenary session. Many fascinating proposals resulted and the advisers thanked us on their departure for the 'learning experience' which they had shared with us. As a direct result of the workshop Mr Harrison and 20 pupils have formed a company and have negotiated a loan with a local bank. Following an intensive marketing exercise they are now successfully selling what I understand they call "protection policies" to local tradesmen. We now have far fewer complaints from neighbourhood shopkeepers on such grounds as theft and vandalism etc.

2.7 As is customary in the Autumn term we were due to have two student teachers from the local college with us for five weeks. Mr Burroughs sadly discovered within days that he was not cut out for teaching and is now, I understand, recovering well from his breakdown. Ms Thompson proved to be a much hardier variety and brought a breath of fresh air to the staffroom. We did have a few complaints from some parents about her unusual approach to sex education but I am assured by her tutors that this degree of frankness is now much encouraged in progressive circles. We have always had a close relationship with the local college and we look forward to this continuing in the years ahead. I have person-ally been pleased to lead three seminars on their Education Management Diploma this term which were entitled 'Team Building in a Time of Contraction',' Ten Decisive Ways to Handle Conflict Situations' and 'Personal Stress Manage-ment for Headteachers'.

TIME WASTING

Time wasting is a bit like bad breath. We are all very quick to spot it in others but we need a good friend to make us aware that we share the affliction. I am very conscious of people who waste my time but I doubt very much if I am half as aware of the ways in which I waste the time of others. This article is written in this spirit. It presents a guide for headteachers on how to waste other people's time as well as their own in the possibly forlorn hope that some of the points will strike home to the extent of making heads a little less prone to this besetting sin.

1. On The Telephone
● No matter how complicated the issue it's always better to telephone than to put it in writing: if it's not on paper it can't be used against you in evidence later and anyway your thoughts on the issue may clarify in the course of talking to Fred. Never try to plan calls in advance: that will only take away your natural gift of spontaneity.

● While you're on the phone don't forget to ask Fred how his daughter is getting on now: your staff like to know you're taking a friendly interest in their lives and anyway you'll certainly be telling Fred how your own daughter is doing.

● Never keep objects like a note book or a pen by the phone: your callers will always warm to your human qualities as you tell them to hold while you search around for these implements: you're a real live breathing human being not an answerphone.

● Encourage your secretary to scrawl down on paper any messages that come in while you're out: it's so satisfying psychologically to crumple up the ones you don't want to respond to and practice your basketball skills trying to lob them into the waste bin.

● Blame your secretary if you discover next week you did want to respond to one of them after all: it's her job now to hunt up the missing number.

● Never indicate to your secretary in advance which calls you don't want putting through to you and don't fix times when no phone calls are to come through under any circumstances: since when have you been worried about interruptions? A bit of a natter over the phone is a welcome relief from paper pushing at any time of the day. It might even give you an excuse to leave unfinished that particularly knotty problem you wish you didn't have to grapple with anyway.

● Should someone come into the room while you're on the phone, just beckon them to take a seat no matter how long the call is likely to take: they can sit and admire your ability to pull funny faces and you can also indicate by inventive gestures what kind of a numbskull you consider this caller to be.

● When they've enjoyed one performance like this, give them an encore by ringing somebody else before you come to their problem: they'll really love to watch your acting skills this one more time.

Chairing Senior Management Team (SMT) Meetings
● Never produce an agenda in advance.

● Spend some time at the beginning of every meeting discussing what are the issues of the day. You're bound to discover some if you chat long enough.

● Call meetings of the whole SMT whenever something crops up you think you might need advice on. Don't take any decisions by yourself if you can avoid it. There's safety in numbers if things go wrong later.

● If it's something you think is really urgent, tell the SMT members to drop everything else they might have scheduled for this evening.

● Wait for the last person to arrive before starting the meeting even if he or she is late.

● Turn up late yourself: they'll surely understand a busy man like you can get side tracked at the last moment by other events.

● Seize the opportunity to have a chat with Bill or Jane that doesn't concern the others: you don't know when you might catch them again.

● If the meeting is taking place in your own room, never take your phone off the hook: one of the calls that comes through might be more important than the issues you are discussing in the meeting. You won't know whether or not this is the case until you've chatted to the caller for a bit.

● Don't bother to take a record of the decisions reached or the actions to be taken by named individuals: half the fun of the next meeting will be remembering what you decided last time and who was supposed to do what with whom.

● Don't set a specific time limit for the meeting: how can you be expected to tell in advance how long it's going to take?

● Don't bother about keeping to the issues of the day: it's important to let members sound off about their pet hobby-horses whenever they want to. These meetings are social occasions and group therapy sessions.

Decision-making

● Make sure your door is always open: no visitor is unwelcome as far as you are concerned. Asking parents, for example, to make appointments in advance is a very unfriendly way to carry on.

● Strive to be as popular as possible by pleasing everyone: they'll love to keep coming back for more.

● Always agree with the last person to see you: you've no idea how many of your staff will want to come crowding in just before decision time if you work on this basis.

● Avoid any unpleasant decisions: you're only going to upset someone. Keep the unpleasant and/or incomprehensible memos perpetually in the in-tray so that you can take them out on a regular basis to remind yourself of all the awful things you've managed to escape from so far. You never know:- the fourth time you read one it might just make sense! Having your in-tray full to overflowing is also a useful device for signalling to your staff how hard you have to work.

● If your in-tray literally does overflow then just add some more paper to the other piles already on your desk. From time to time re-arrange these piles together with the post-it stickers which you put there to remind you what was urgent last week etc. so that they are more aesthetically pleasing; it beats flower arrangement as therapy any day. Never under any circumstances throw any incoming junk mail straight into the bin until you have very carefully considered whether it might not come in handy some day.

● Avoid any complicated decisions: you might make a mistake. Wait until you're absolutely sure you're taking the right decision that none of your staff can possibly criticise. Never do today what you can put off until the day after tomorrow.

● If you're finally driven to answer one of these awkward memos before you are sure of the correct answer, try and fudge your response so that nobody will be really sure what you think. That way nobody can hold you responsible if things go wrong.

● Never refuse requests for assistance even if you've already got far too many tasks to do: saying no can give offence, but you might try the odd mumbled "maybe" or "perhaps". If you are forced to say yes, they'll probably forget later on that you promised to do it anyway: you certainly will.

● Firmly resolve to go on believing anyone who comes to your room saying that he or she only needs a few minutes of your time.

● If any of your staff come to see you not on the above "few minutes of time" basis, offer them a cup of coffee (your secretary just loves to make coffee all day) and give them a comfortable chair to sit in: they'll probably find plenty of things to talk about even if there was very little on their agendas to start with.

● Never be the first to stand up or to indicate there might be other pressing things you have to do: it's so impolite to keep looking at your watch, for example. You can't be too careful with your body language. It would never do to convey the impression that you're impatient.

● Never prioritise your decisions: far be it from you to class some things as trivial.

● The deadlines of others are meant to be broken: you mustn't allow time constraints to prevent you doing the job entirely to your own satisfaction. Never let the good be the enemy of the best. You keep on taking a pride in being a perfectionist. As far as you are concerned you are writing your memos for posterity.

● Never set a precedent: if any member of staff comes to you with a novel idea, always look through the rule book in detail to see if there's some excuse for taking no action. If you can't find anything to stop it outright, set up a large working party of pressed men and women to consider it in detail. They've probably got nothing better to do.

● Never delegate: there's nobody who could do the job half as well as you. Just think what would happen if somebody else made a mess of it. Never mind if you haven't got time to tackle it yourself for the moment, they'll just have to wait until you can get around to it.

● Take as much paperwork home as you can manage to transfer from your desk to your briefcase: you've probably taken some of the same papers home two or three times already but it makes you feel better if you carry them backwards and forwards a few times. Those who are waiting for decisions should be grateful for the attention you are giving to their paperwork.

A TACTICAL GUIDE TO SURVIVING THE INSPECTION PROCESS

Conferences and seminars are proliferating on the new inspections of schools. Many headteachers have already come a cropper at the very first hurdle in this new spectacular handicap chase sponsored by the manufacturers of other well known board games such as 'The Grand National Curriculum', 'League Table Mania' and 'Opting Out Monopoly'. This first hurdle 'merely' consisted of obtaining a copy of the new National Hunt Rules entitled 'The Handbook for the Inspection of Schools'. This production, in a ring binder format instantly familiar to the aficionados of the many other games produced by this firm in recent years, was a snip at £15.

Many of the punters, of course, soon realised that these first editions, with their built-in obsolesence, very quickly become collectors' items, and this particular printing sold out almost as soon as it hit the market. Those heads who missed the first day issue were dismayed to find that both OFSTED and the DFE responded with all the warmth of the speaking clock to assure telephone callers on this subject that it was now out of print but that an additional printing would appear in due course.

To anyone familiar with the ways of Elizabeth House and Sanctuary Buildings this could only mean one thing, and there was then a mad scramble to obtain places on the new inspectorate training courses where a copy of the handbook could still be obtained at cost price. This indicates that it is really intended not for heads but for the Dad's Army of an inspectorate hastily gathered together ready for the invasion of schools. An alternative guide to inspection survival is clearly needed for heads, hence the following hurriedly produced starter kit.

Who are these people who are going to inspect your school in the near future? You are aware that the Education Bill in which all this was incorporated was going through parliament at a time when the Conservative Party actually thought it might for once stand an outside chance of losing a looming election. For this reason alone, some of the more obvious right wing lunacies were avoided. The raiding parties will not now consist only of those with absolutely no previous connection with education whatsoever. To the sea-green incorruptibles of the counter-revolution this means that many of the more dubious categories of the *ancien regime* are infiltrating into the ranks. It is even rumoured that some of the teacher educators from higher education, applying under assumed names, of course, and stating their professions as butcher, gun-runner, candlestick-maker and the like, are finding convenient priest holes in this inspectorate ahead of the final drive to eliminate all those still holding to the progressive faith.

Ex-HMIs (Her Majesty's Inspectors) have not, therefore, been barred from participation because they had joined the think tank black lists of those suspected of still doubting whether Mr. Gradgrind was indeed the very model of a model mentor-teacher. Indeed ex-HMI are to some extent serving as the trainers of the new cadres, rather in the way that survivors of the trenches were sought to instruct the Home Guard at the start of Hitler's War. Fortunately, the efficacy of that earlier example of crash training was never put to the test but there is unlikely to be an Operation Barbarossa to divert attention from the Western Front this time around. So ask for the CVs of your inspectors as soon as their names are communicated to you.

Start with the CV of the Registered Inspector, but carefully follow up all the clues these CVs provide. (It is worth noting, in passing, that Registered Inspectors, Team Inspectors and Lay Inspectors are, despite their very differing needs, all going through pretty much the same emergency training course, and it will be helpful if you can sign on for one of these yourself so that you can the more easily spot the training inadequacies of the shock troops assigned to your school.)

If your school budget will run to it, hire a private detective to find the truths which might lie behind the CVs. Is Z an ex-headteacher because (a) she is now 93? (b) she was encouraged to take early retirement after that unfortunate incident on the school trip to the Matterhorn? (c) her school was closed due to financial mismanagement? Is Q really a model? Does J's past history of simultaneously having been a governor at six schools imply that he might have certain political leanings? Is it really only ten years since any of the inspecting team last taught in a classroom?

Before the inspection week at the school begins, there will be an official parents' meeting which it is the responsibility of the chairman of governors to arrange. This is strictly for parents only, and you are expressly barred as it is well known that parents are intimidated by your presence because of your powers to hold their offspring as hostages. This may look like the beginning of the end to you because you are well aware of the propensity of Mrs Jenkins and her cronies to dish the dirt on the school behind your back. Do not despair. If you have been wise enough to line up a few 'trusties' as parent governors, you're probably ok, because they are allowed to attend, and they can position themselves near the well known trouble makers.

If your trusties have been well chosen they will be sufficiently 'heavy' to cause panic in the ranks when photographs of the children of these potential dissidents are ostentatiously passed from one parent governor to another. It is not essential to have marked these photographs with large black crosses, but it might help to promote the kind of impression you wish to create. Failing this, encourage those of your staff on whom you can rely for support, and who have children of school age of their own, to register them as pupils of your school immediately. This then gives these teachers the automatic right to attend the meeting. If enough of your teachers have been fertile they may well out-number the other parents present.

Furthermore you can try to persuade your chairman of gover-nors to repeat his crowd-pulling act at the last annual general meeting of parents and governors when the governors were able to surround the small handful of stragglers who had wandered in thinking it was a bingo night. (The only problem there is that you are supposed to inform the inspectors how many parents turned up that night. There's another creative puzzle for you to solve.)

You will be asked by the Registered Inspector to supply appro-priate documentation before the inspection week begins. Some of this paperwork may surprise you. You may not have kept any records at all of meetings of your Senior Management Team. (The way you run your school, the last thing you would want is written evidence of the decisions taken behind closed doors.) Indeed you may never have had anything remotely resembling a Senior Management Team. Again, do not fall into the slough of despond. You've no doubt heard of the Hitler Diaries, and you don't have anyone half as clued up as Hugh Trevor-Roper/Lord Dacre to fool.

Start writing the fictitious minutes of these imaginary meetings now. Provided you use suitably aged paper, nobody will be any the wiser. If any members of staff should catch sight of these documents, they will probably think they slept through this or that meeting which they can't recollect attending. Some of your staff must have left during the period you are now trying to reconstruct. Write their fabricated contributions to meetings in such a way that they can be held fully responsible for any of the more obvious catastrophes of the past few years. When the inspectors question you about these events, imply that your powers of persuasion are nothing short of legendary when it comes to getting the incompetent and the downright crooked to tender their resignations. You can throw caution to the winds if you've been fortunate enough to have some of your pedagogues pass on to that eternally happy staffroom in the sky. They are the obvious scapegoats for anything that might lead to a spell of hard labour at Her Majesty's expense.

During the inspection week make it very obvious to the inspectors that they are also being inspected. Walk round the school with a notebook, and mutter aloud as you make jottings when inspectors pass by. Some of these new inspectors are very insecure indeed. This may have been their first gainful employment in years, and they are aware that a bad word to OFSTED could mean they will never be part of a successful tender again. Instruct the staff to note as pointedly as possible the time of entry and departure from lessons of the inspectors. Remark jocularly to some of the more nervous looking of their brethren that you understand that the DFE is having some considerable difficulty getting anyone to undertake the inspection of certain schools and you're not one bit surprised.

After the inspection report arrives be prepared for the local journalists to pick up on the criticisms, sensationalising them as only they know how. Have a press release quickly prepared which stresses all the elements of praise in the report. (There have to be some!) Don't look for any help on how to remedy deficiencies from the report itself. That's now your problem, or to be more accurate the responsibility of your governing body which now has to produce a plan setting out the specific action it intends to take in response to the report. But guess who's going to have to write this on the governors' behalf yet again? Don't forget when writing this that you are legally obliged to send copies to Mrs Jenkins and her parents' coven, along with anyone else living within three miles radius of the school who requests a copy. That should just about use up the whole of your reprography budget.

So that's filled in the odd Tuesday morning for you. How are you possibly going to find enough other jobs to while away the rest of the week?

HOW TO RUIN MEETINGS OF GOVERNING BODIES

Part I: The Bad Chairman's Checklist

1.0 Before the meeting

1.1 Never fix the date of the next meeting at the end of the previous meeting.

1.2 Give inadequate notice of the next meeting.

1.3 Decide you need to hold a meeting next week and phone around to see if you can find a time when at least some of the Governing Body can make it.

1.4 Don't issue an agenda in advance.

1.5 Don't produce any papers in advance.

2.0 At the start of the meeting

2.1 Assume others will arrive late.

2.2 Arrive late yourself.

2.3 Never start on time under any circumstances.

2.4 If by some unforeseen chance everybody does arrive on time,then spend the first few minutes in social chit chat.

2.5 Teach the lesson that punctuality is the thief of time.

3.0 Getting the meeting underway

3.1 Leave the seating arrangements as they were for the social chit chat.

3.2 Let those who are smoking carry on doing so, but do not provide ashtrays.

3.3 Do not set a time limit to the meeting.

3.4 Discuss what the agenda might be.

3.5 Do not encourage anyone to write out an agreed agenda for himself or herself.

3.6 Ask for a volunteer to clerk the meeting.

3.7 Say you're not really looking for detailed minutes but just a brief record of the meeting in general.

3.8 When no volunteers are forthcoming say it doesn't really matter as you can write up a record yourself after the meeting.

4.0 Once the meeting is underway

4.1 Pass round the handwritten scrawl you made yourself as a record of the last meeting.

4.2 Assume everybody agrees with your version of events.

4.3 Ask if anyone has any matters arising.

4.4 Start the main agenda with some trivial items that can be nevertheless guaranteed to raise tempers and waste considerable time. (A good standby is to begin with the problems you had parking your car in a convenient place and to ask if other governors had similar problems.)

4.5 When you finally get around to the main reason you called the meeting in the first place give a lengthy oral summary of the detailed LEA circular that you haven't photocopied and circulated in advance.

4.6 Assume that you have summarised correctly and that   everyone has understood your summary.

4.7 Answer the telephone call from your spouse about the arrangements for your meeting in the restaurant later in the evening.

4.8 Go back to the meeting by asking: "Where were we?"

5.0 As the meeting progresses

5.1 Get into a dialogue with the most vocal governor (besides yourself that is).

5.2 Refer to the discussion the two of you have already had over the telephone about the main issue.

5.3 Hint by the odd wink etc. that the two of you have come to some agreements that you don't want to discuss openly.

5.4 Ignore the governors who appear to have nothing to say.

5.5 Quickly interrupt anyone who shows signs of wanting to take a different line to the one you have already decided is the right one.

6.0 Closing the meeting

6.1 Look at your watch. Say: "my goodness is that the time?"

6.2 Sum up by saying that a clear consensus exists as to the action to be taken and there is, therefore, no need to take a vote.

6.3 Close the meeting by telling a joke you heard that morning and by asking the headteacher when the coffee is coming.

6.4 Don't fix a date for the next meeting.

HOW TO RUIN MEETINGS OF GOVERNING BODIES
PART II: THE HEADTEACHER'S CHECKLIST

1.0 Before the meeting

1.1 Never send out your headteacher's report in advance of the meeting.

1.2 Do the report in a handwritten form. (If anyone queries at the meeting why it isn't typed, claim that the school secretary can't cope with the normal workload without your adding to it. Add that you're not going to start learning clerical skills yourself. Make a joke about this still being the age of the quill pen as far as you are concerned.)

1.3 Make sure the photocopies you produce make the writing even more illegible.

1.4 In case anyone can still read the report, make sure it as dull and bland as possible.

1.5 Start the report with a lengthy section on the 'fabric of the building'. Detail for the nth. time the catalogue of LEA neglect which has left the school in its present parlous position. Put forward no concrete proposals for action.

1.6 Under the heading of 'curriculum' simply state that the National Curriculum is being implemented according to Government requirements despite the enormous extra workload that this is thrusting onto your already overburdened shoulders. (On no account give any details of exactly what changes in the school curriculum the introduction of the National Curriculum has occasioned.)

1.7 If an unusually high number of teachers are leaving the school, stress the excellent training they have received for posts elsewhere and emphasise the importance of 'new blood' on the school staff and the dangers of stagnation.

1.8 If not a single teacher is leaving, point to this as evidence that you all work together as one big happy family. Argue that the teamwork you have developed can only be enhanced by the stability in staffing which is the envy of all the other schools in the area.

1.9 If a couple of teachers are leaving, point to the crucial need to maintain a balance between stagnation and chaotic staff turnover. Imply that other schools in the area fall into one or other of these traps. (It is difficult to imply that any one school is falling into both traps simultaneously but it might be worth a try.)

1.10 If pupil intakes are increasing, argue that this is convincing proof of the efficacy of your headship and the popularity of the school.

1.11 If school rolls are falling, argue that the nature of the area is such that the birth rate is in steep decline. (Note that this is equally effective as an argument in middle class areas and in working class ones. In the former you should argue that the high cost of mortgages means that the young householders can't afford to start families. In the latter you should imply that the sexual act is no longer undertaken for purposes of procreation. In both cases your Governors will, in the main, feel superior, either morally or financially, as they are likely to be parents themselves. With a bit of luck this passage in your report should encourage them to go on at length during the meeting about the declining state of the nation. This will distract their attention from things about which they might do something positive.

2.0 At the start of the meeting

2.1 Do not set out the staff room for the meeting in any systematic fashion.

2.2 As the Governors arrive, tell them to grab a chair and pull it up to the others.

2.3 Carry on writing at a table in the corner. (This creates the impression that you are overworked and find this meeting a useless further imposition on your working day.)

2.4 Make the atmosphere generally as unwelcoming as possible.

2.5 Only join the group once the chairman calls the meeting to order. Make some joke along the lines of: 'My, aren't we getting formal these days!'.

2.6 Sit next to someone who can be guaranteed to laugh at your asides during the meeting.

3.0 During the meeting

3.1 On any other issues than the ones you have raised in your own report make sure you are not seen as giving a lead. That is the chairman's job as far as you are concerned.

3.2 Undermine the leads the chairman does give. Make frequent jocular asides which make the chairman seem pompous.

3.3 Argue against the setting up of sub-committees on such matters as curriculum, finance etc. on the grounds that they will only occasion a lot more meetings which will be a waste of everyone's time.

3.4 If you are asked about recent DFE and LEA circulars say you haven't the resources to reproduce them but that you'll read them and summarise them when you can get around to it.

3.5 If your attitudes to pupils are questioned by one of the older Governors suggest that the speaker doesn't know what youngsters are like these days.

3.6 If the speaker is a Parent Governor imply that s(he) is adopting a partisan approach designed to favour his\her own children.

3.7 Assert that any visits to classrooms will not be seen by teachers as laudable attempts on the part of Governors to familiarise themselves with pupils etc. but merely as a form of snooping.

3.8 When it comes to your own report, if by any chance the

section on the fabric of the building has not put everybody to sleep, go into nauseating detail about the toilets that won't flush.

3.9 If asked about such things as development plans, job descriptions etc. suggest that these are merely new-fangled jargon for notions you've been carrying around in your head for years.

3.10 Resist any attempts to invite members of staff to come to Governing Body meetings to discuss their areas of responsibility. Say they're far too busy to find time for that.

4.0 After the meeting

4.1 Try to make sure that Governors leave their copies of your report in the waste paper basket so that you won't have points quoted against you in future.

4.2 Insist that the next meeting, like all the previous ones, must take place immediately after the end of the school day.

4.3 Try to get everyone off the premises as soon as possible. Suggest that the caretaker wants to lock the place up and get home.

HOW TO RUIN MEETINGS OF GOVERNING BODIES

PART III:THE PARENT GOVERNOR'S CHECKLIST

1.0 Before the meeting
1.1 Never read the minutes of the previous meeting before attending the next one.
1.2 Ignore background papers for the meeting.
1.3 Read the date and time of the meeting on the agenda and ignore the rest.
1.4 Spend no time before the meeting considering the main issues that are to be discussed and what you might contribute to the discussion.

2.0 At the start of the meeting
2.1 Arrive late.
2.2 Apologise profusely saying you have just too many things on your plate to fit them all in at the right times.

2.3 Create a disturbance looking for a seat.

2.4 Fiddle around in your bag as obtrusively as possible looking for your papers.

2.5 Ask your neighbour if you can borrow a biro.

2.6 Start to smoke and blow smoke over everyone else.

3.0 During the meeting

3.1 Talk to every topic even if you have nothing worthwhile to say.

3.2 When the discussion moves from one item to another, raise a point about the last item.

3.3 If the meeting is on the verge of reaching a decision, wait until the last moment before expressing a contrary view.

3.4 Interrupt others when you disagree with them.

3.5 Repeat at length those points made by others with which you agree. Constantly say 'we' to imply that you have wide support for your views.

3.6 If there is any danger of a silence, break in immediately.

3.7 Never make constructive criticisms. Remember that all criticism should be negative and, if possible, bad-tempered.

3.8 Try to avoid giving praise or appreciation of the contributions of others.

3.9 Better still, don't pay attention to the contributions of others unless you want to score points off them.

3.10 Try to make others feel inadequate.

3.11 Waste time on issues that are off the track of the present discussion.

3.12 Think of as many reasons as possible why the solutions to problems that are offered won't work.

3.13 Talk across the room to another parent governor. If this is criticised from the chair, then wink, raise your eyebrows, smirk etc.

3.14 When tasks are being handed out, keep quiet, look at the floor etc. Never volunteer, but be ready to criticise the efforts of those who do.

3.15 Write something that has clearly nothing to do with the meeting: a letter is usually enough to show your lack of interest in the present issue.

3.16 If this does not appear to be irritating people enough, then yawn, look at your watch or look out of the window.

3.17 Alternatively, mutter under your breath, tap your

fingers on the table, or shuffle your feet.

3.18 Write notes to be passed around the room to your parent governor friend.

3.19 Never give way or change your mind because of what others say. If the arguments appear to have gone against you, then insist on a vote.

4.0 At the end of the meeting

4.1 Raise some issues concerning your own children under 'Any Other Business'.

4.2 Make sure nobody has been alerted to these in advance.

4.3 Demand to know what is going to be done about your grievances.

4.4 As soon as these issues have been dealt with (and you have made it clear that this has not been done to your satisfaction), leave before the date and time of the next meeting are fixed. Never stay behind to help with the clearing up.

ALL THINGS TO ALL PEOPLE

t is only in recent years (though it already seems like an age) that we have had a National Curriculum in England and Wales. It is, therefore, fair to say that we ought to know what the current dominant expectation is at national level of what should be taught in state schools for at least a good part of the school day. (The fact that in reality there is often still considerable confusion is a condemnation of the botched way in which the National Curriculum was launched.) It is, nevertheless, much less clear what the national expectation is of the nature of the school as an organisation.

Yet if we are to manage effectively, we need to know what the nature of the organisation should be before we can decide upon the criteria for judging the effectiveness of particular schools. To take two extreme examples, if we think that a school should be organised as 'one big happy family' we may well have very different criteria for effectiveness than if, in our view, schools should be run along military lines. These examples may be extreme, but they should not be dismissed as fanciful. Many a headteacher of a small primary school will talk about the family atmosphere of the school, and will do so with a great deal more public credibility than bosses of large companies who are still quite likely to use the 'one big happy family' metaphor for their organisations. (I came across another lamentably implausible example of the latter in a popular magazine only this week.)

At possibly the other end of the spectrum, military academies do still exist, but in a much more widespread sense there was a time which extended from the Second World War until at least the end of National Service at the start of the 1960s when many an all-boys secondary school in the UK had a 'military' managerial ethos. As I then perceived it, on the giving and the receiving ends, this owed a great deal to notions of organisation which the majority of the staff had personally encountered in the armed services at a very formative stage of their lives. Nor should we necessarily assume that this military ethos disappeared completely with the demise of National Service.

A researcher in Portugal, Rui Gomes of Lisbon University, has recently suggested, in work not yet published in English, that there are at least four different current expectations of what the dominant culture of secondary schools should be in his own country. Taking this, very loosely, as my starting point, I will now go on to argue that all shrewd headteachers should be aware of the probability that there will be these differing expectations of their schools as organisations. The trick will be to match their presentation to the audience. To some extent this has always been the case. Many a boys, boarding school headteacher faced with a parent from a very obvious military background (to continue my previous organisational analogy) will have talked about "running a very tight ship", "keeping the troops in order", "going over the top" and so on.

This then is the expedient headteacher's guide to spotting and responding to the organisational expectations of others, and I will start with that fairly recent, but very pushy, newcomer to the scene: the view of the school as a **business enterprise**. The frame of reference here is decidedly economic. Remember that you are not expected to be concerned about children as children but as potential or actual age-weighted cash units. The real clients or customers of your educational emporium are not, in any case, the pupils but their parents.

What do parents who view the school as a business enterprise want? They clearly want results. This means, in their terms, high examination success rates; and never forget that their terms are your terms. The customers in this kind of enterprise are king and queen, and aces and jacks to boot. To present such parents with the appropriate prospectus you may need to massage the figures by preventing the weaker brethren from ever taking the examinations in the first place.

This, of course, is going to cause you some difficulties with the parents who view the school as a benevolent society designed to give all pupils in its care every opportunity, however remote, of success. Such conflicts are sadly inevitable in a pluralist society. The whole point of this guide is to convince the expedient head of the need to adopt different roles with different audiences. I will not insult the reader's intelligence by dwelling in each case upon the correct ways to avoid role conflict, but just as an example in this instance, you will need to talk to those who believe in the benevolent society approach about the damning effects of failure on the child's psyche. Much better that your little charges are shielded from the buffeting of nature's crueller elements, and given a stable and protective start in life etc.

To return, however, to the school as business enterprise, you will constantly refer to your staff as the management team. There will be junior and senior executives, of course, but you are all determined, to a man or a woman, to make your school the most efficient outfit of its kind in the area. You will measure your productivity principally by the aforementioned examination results, but any other equivalent prizes to the Queen's Awards will be competed for ferociously.

You will have a number of sliding panels on your headteacher's (or better chief executive's) office walls which are interchangeable at the press of various buttons. In the case of the business enterprise audience the correct button to press is the one which brings up the panels with the cost-effectiveness and productivity charts.

Closely related to the view of the school as a business enterprise is the view of the school as a **public relations (PR) firm**. In this case it is public opinion that rules supreme to the extent that success will be measured by the extent of the 'good' media coverage the school receives. No edition of the local rag should go out without some favourable mention of the school. Photo-opportunities are a must. Pupils and staff should be dressed up in weird and wonderful outfits for ever more unlikely reasons so that front page photographs are assured. Reporters should be wined and dined, and press releases devised which can be converted into news coverage by these reporters with the minimum of effort on their part. Try to produce stories that will attract radio and television coverage. Local coverage is good but national coverage is better.

But always remember that your PR firm is only concerned with good news. In your business it is simply not true that all news is good news. Your clientele do not want to hear that three of your teachers were assaulted last week by pupils. Point out to these troublemaking staff that their jobs depend on the school's reputation and hush such affairs up. Never call in the police or press criminal charges. You could make the front page of the *News of the Planet* for all the wrong reasons.

It becomes a little more difficult if your science labs. are torched over the week-end. Such news has an unfortunate habit of leaking out. But you could always claim it was the result of an industrial accident due to science staff working overtime on a secret and innovative project designed to protect the environment or promote world health. It is up to you to put a positive public image forward at all times. There are no problems or difficulties, only challenges and opportunities. Any of the awards won by your school (and you will force your staff and pupils to enter every competition that's going) will be emblazoned on your school notepaper, and on the commercially designed signs scattered around the school and its environs.

Remember that any outfit can have a colourful and attractive heraldic crest complete with Latin tag which will suggest to the gullible that the school was founded by a wandering group of Benedictine monks in the fourteenth century. The name of the school is critical. If you don't like being referred to as 'Sludgeville Secondary', then opt out of the LEA, bung the local vicar a few readies and call yourself 'St. Paul's Grant Maintained School for the Sons and Daughters of Gentlefolk' if you think that will bring in the punters.

The correct button to push in your study this time is the one which brings up the panels with the holiday brochure photographs of the West Wing of the school, complete with ornamental fish pond, on the one day in the year when the sun's rays penetrated the industrial smog.

Somewhat out of fashion at present is the view of the school as a **citizens' advice bureau**. In this model the school is there to impart the information that will make the pupils into worthy recipients of citizens' charters about all kinds of public services including education.

Viewed in this light teachers are public servants with contracts to provide a cheap and cheerful, but nonetheless reliable service for the good townsfolk of the parish. They are one more organ of the body politic which must function as a healthy living organism in the national interest. The nation will be best served if its children are provided with equal opportunities to display their talents and their merit to the full. This will be a classless society in which the promotion of national unity and consensus will be the main *raison d'être* of the schools. The advent of this new spirit of togetherness across the land will herald a new age of unparalleled national achievement.

The relevant wall panels to bring up in the executive suite will be tasteful line drawings of the Palace of Westminster and the local town hall, but experience suggests that this is a button you won't have to push very often. Recent surveys suggest that there is only one human being left in the whole realm who actually thinks that anyone else believes in this scenario of civic virtue any more, and his position as Prime Minister seems decidedly dodgy.

Let's end this scenic tour of organisational expectations by returning to the view of the school as a **happy family**. The expectation here is that the school will be a very model of domestic harmony. Teachers will be expected to act *in loco parentis* and nothing less than the education of the whole child will suffice. Team games will be extolled for their character forming virtues rather than for their potential for supplying the school with trophies. It's playing a straight bat that matters here. Whether you win or lose is immaterial. It is at least as important to inculcate moral and spiritual values as it is to impart knowledge. The process is of no less significance than the product. The object here is not to produce 'clever devils' but to turn out into the world well-rounded individuals who will enhance the worlds in which they go on to live and move and have their being.

Teachers will be expected to be firm but fair to their pupils. They will view each other as colleagues and friends. Hierarchical relationships in this learning organisation will be kept to a minimum. The school is a community which is a microcosm of the wider community outside in which individuals are bound together by ties of friendship and loyalty.

'Image' is something which stems from the reality of the relationships in the organisation not a decorated fig-leaf to conceal that reality. And so on.... but the problem for the headteachers who are responding to such expectations (and it is just remotely possible that they hold such beliefs themselves) is that many of the very people who profess to hold such assumptions have quietly discarded them some time ago.

The domestic model of the family as displayed in TV commercials and on the backs of corn flake packets is less evident on the actual UK doorstep. The extended family may be considered to be alive and well and living in such Elysian fields as those in an English writer's rose-coloured spectacle view of Provence, but it doesn't seem to be doing too well in an urban Britain with the second highest divorce rate in Europe etc. No amount of panels in the headteacher's study showing pictures of happy scenes in the daily life of the school will obscure the fact that much of the world outside, with its rapidly increasing number of broken homes, is not like that any more. It will possibly only be a minority of the parents who hold these sorts of expectations any longer.

So what does the poor headteacher do when faced simultaneously with all these different 'client groups' on say the annual speech day. Well here is where my new dial-a-text service comes into its own. For a very reasonable fee we can supply ready made speeches which contain enough metaphors from each of these scenarios to keep all the punters happy. Never forget the lesser known law of Abe Lincoln that you can fool all of the people some of the time. The politicians only have to pull off this trick once every five years or so. You may have to manage this at least once a year, but don't despair. People's memories are short and selective. At the time of your speech they will only pay attention to the metaphors that tie in with their own expectations. A year later they will have completely forgotten your words of wisdom and our latest dial-a-text will have sufficient topical references to hide the fact that the sentiments are practically identical with those of yesteryear.

It is, however, best to avoid the audio-visual effects, because people do pay attention to pictures after years of serious training in this respect, and slides of all the various panels in your office might cause some uneasy reflections in your audience. The Vicar of Bray stuck to sermons and so should you.

WHEN THE GOING GETS TOUGH

We are all told these days that the management of change is the name of the game as far as the educational scene is concerned. That may well be so considering the frenetic pace of government intervention in educa tional management, but there is some evidence that the rules of the game may be different for some than for others. Here is the alternative handbook on the subject.

1.0 Implement change only after a crisis occurs.
1.1 Don't plan ahead and prepare for change - that only wastes time. Wait until the system breaks down before you start to think of another one. If it ain't bust, don't fix it. Fire-fighting is a good deal more exciting than administering preventive medicine.
1.2 Don't anticipate the problems there might be in implementing the change - that way you'll only get cold feet about

carrying it out.

1.3 Don't allocate financial resources in advance - scrapping the old to bring in the new will free up some cash anyway.

1.4 Don't worry about the time required of staff to learn the new techniques involved - they'll just have to put in some more unpaid overtime.

2.0 Don't help people to accept change.

2.1 Don't discuss the change with them - this only gives them a chance to gripe. (For the same reason you've regarded the 'suggestions box' as a joke for years.) Consultation and participation are frills you can't spare the time for. You're fighting a fire, not running an armchair debating society. There's no point in trying to make them think they have any 'ownership' of this innovation anyway. You make it clear from the start this is 'top down' not 'bottom up'.

2.2 You know where you want to bolt to now the crisis has occurred. (This is what you call vision.) They're just going to have to follow. The last thing you want is a collaborative culture where the participants build a vision together. There's always the offchance that way you might end up having to go somewhere you don't like.

2.3 Steal some trite company motto such as: "Our aim is a quality service for our customers." Describe this as a "mission statement". Make this a heading on every conceivable document you produce. Don't bother to explain who you have in mind as your customers. Anyone who asks for such analysis is too clever by half and obviously a stirrer. The one thing you are clear about is that your own staff certainly aren't your customers.

2.4 Don't try to allay the fears of the potential losers: as far as you're concerned they can all be losers - this change is going ahead whether they like it or not.

2.5 Don't try to stress the potential benefits and opportunities, most of them you've got lined up for yourself in any case. Play on their fears - the threats to their job security, to their hard won skills and to their general professional pride are quite enough to keep them on their toes.

2.6 Reduce their ability to resist the change by undermining any collective bargaining procedures they possess.

3.0 Once the change has been introduced.

3.1 Ok that's it. Leave them to get on with it. Ongoing staff development and assistance are luxuries you can't afford.

3.2 Treat all complaints about the way the change is going as whinging.

3.3 Don't try to lead by example - it's your staff who have to make the adjustments not you.

3.4 Have no sympathy with those who find it difficult to learn new skills.

3.5 Ignore any obvious signs of stress. They've got GPs haven't they? All they need to do is keep on taking the tablets. Take a very hard line on any absenteeism. Show them you'll have no truck with scrimshankers.

3.6 Don't have any systematic monitoring procedures to check on how the innovation is going - the whingers and the toadies will give you all the information you need. This also helps to destroy any chance of group co-operation or solidarity - they would only use that solidarity to wreck the change anyway.

4.0 If you think that the innovation is faltering or even showing signs of floundering.

4.1 Make some more adjustments in exactly the same way you introduced the innovation in the first place. Don't bother about consistency of direction - veering off at a tangent might be just the trick you need. When in trouble: duck, bob and weave. If this fails, then hide.

4.2 Set up an internal hunt for scapegoats. Blame the victims. Create a general panic. That should get their adrenalin flowing. It'll give you a much-needed buzz in any case.

4.3 Claim to the external audience that troublemakers have spread rumours that were scurrilous distortions of the true picture. "Crisis? What crisis?"

4.4 Make a few examples of those you see as barrack room lawyers in order to encourage the others.

4.5 Demand more time and effort from everybody but yourself. Paste up posters with slogans such as: "When the going gets tough, it's the tough that get going." Tear down all the posters with slogans such as: "You don't have to be mad to work here, but it helps."

5.0 If it looks definitely like failing after all.

5.1 Get out while the going's good. Chances are you could be well away from the scene of the massacre by the time it occurs.

5.2 Claim everything was going fine while you were there. If only you hadn't had to go on to that even more demanding, albeit more prestigious and more highly paid, job, all would have been well. The staff may be thoroughly demoralised now but morale was sky high in your day.

5.3 Join the general witch hunt against your successor if he or she shows the slightest inclination to cast doubt on your theories or methods. Argue that what was needed was more of the same, not a pussyfooting reluctance to put the boot in when it was required. If a sacrifice is needed to satiate the blood lust of the disappointed and the disillusioned, then don't hesitate to put in a bad word. Lynch mobs rarely question the motives of those who are urging them on.

5.4 Write a book on the theme of: "How to Innovate Successfully".

5.5 Produce a video on the same theme. Lecture widely on the subject.

5.6 Accept a Visiting Professorship at your local university's business school.

5.7 Become the Robert Maxwell Professor of Business Ethics.

THE MINUTES: THE TRUE STORY!

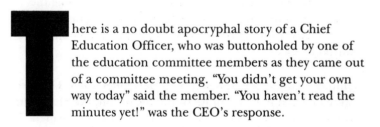here is a no doubt apocryphal story of a Chief Education Officer, who was buttonholed by one of the education committee members as they came out of a committee meeting. "You didn't get your own way today" said the member. "You haven't read the minutes yet!" was the CEO's response.

This is a useful reminder of how far the usual minutes of meetings actually conceal the true nature of the events which took place. Rather remarkably, however, I have recently received, in the proverbial plain brown envelope, an exceptional set of minutes of a school staff meeting which appear to be an attempt to convey not only what actually happened, but some of the motivations of those present as well. After some investigation on my part, I am given to understand that these were produced by the member of staff who had normally clerked these meetings over very many years. On this occasion, however, he was due to take premature retirement on a breakdown pension shortly after the meeting took place. As his own leaving present to the head and the staff he produced this set of minutes which he distributed into the staff pigeon-holes at the end of his last school day. Presumably quite unintentionally, he had forgotten on this one occasion to clear them with the chair before their distribution. I am sure his colleagues will have forgiven him for this small lapse, no doubt brought on by the emotions of the leave-taking. I am now able to bring this unique document to a wider audience. Because of the constraints of the space available to me I am only circulating those parts of the minutes leading up to and including the first substantive item on the agenda. The items omitted here include ones on the school curriculum post-16 and the impending OFSTED inspection of the school. Perhaps we might feature those on another occasion.

SLUDGEVILLE SECONDARY SCHOOL
Minutes of the school staff meeting held on 4 April 1994.
1. Apologies were received from Mr Harris and Mrs Lovejoy who were enjoying one of their many trysts while the head thought they were organising a course and their respective spouses thought they were at the staff meeting. No apologies were received as usual from Mr Johnson who has, like the rest of us, better things to do with his time, but, unlike the rest of us, goes and does them without giving a damn about anybody else.

2. Minutes of the meeting held on 16 December 1993. These were deemed to be accurate by the head from the chair, who once again took a sullen silence from the staff to mean assent. As I wrote the first draft, which was subsequently used by the head as a plot outline on which to base another of his fictional travesties, I wish to signify my dissent at the point of writing these minutes. As a true record of the meeting, I think the heading alone might just about have been allowed to stand.

3. Matters Arising.
3.1. Equipment Inventory.
Mr Stephens was publicly humiliated for having failed to take action on this. The chore was then dumped firmly in the

copious lap of Miss Jenkins.

3.2. Photocopying.

The staff were unanimous, yet again, that the present facilities were inadequate. The head indicated, as usual, that he would offer every possible assistance short of actual help.

3.3. Car Parking.

See 3.2 above as far as 'outcomes' are concerned. The head did not volunteer to give up his own reserved car parking space in an attempt to discover how the rest of us live, in this as in all other respects. (It is worth noting at this point that the above items, which are no nearer resolution now than they were twelve months ago, took up three quarters of an hour of the meeting. This left staff tired and despondent and in no fit state to tackle constructively the substantive items which followed. As this has been the regular pattern of events at these meetings in recent years, I am now convinced that this is exactly what the chair intends to happen.)

4. Relationship of Senior Management Team (SMT) to Staff as a Whole.

The head began by reporting that he had placed this item on the agenda at the request of Mr Jenkins. (This suggests that either Jim Jenkins hasn't been here long enough to know any better and has developed mad newcomers' disease, or that he has become the head's latest trusty and is merely acting as the ventriloquist's dummy. In either case, it is suspicious that this item was not killed at birth by the head as is his wont. What is Herod up to this time?)

Mr Jenkins then spoke to the item by commenting that in his previous school, it had been customary for all staff to receive copies of the minutes of the meetings of the SMT. In comparison he had felt relatively in the dark since his arrival here as there was no such ready access to information at that level. (That's rich! Those of us not on the SMT (as well as some of those who are) have been in the pitch black night of ignorance for years on anything that really matters in this outfit.) Mrs Thompson argued that she had enough to read already, thank you very much, and she was not in favour of further destruction of the rain forests. (It was a revelation to many of us that Mrs Thompson could read anything above the knitting pattern level.) The head said that while he had every sympathy with Mrs

Thompson's ecological concerns, he did not think that circulation of SMT minutes would be a significant contribution to global warming. (So he does want to go public on the SMT! Why?) Ms Desmond said that as the Head of the Physics Department she would feel constrained about discussing delicate issues if her views were going to be minuted and circulated to all staff. (Well that confirms the rumours that she's been dishing the dirt on the staff of her department with the SMT.) The head responded to the effect that the minutes would have to be carefully edited before circulation to ensure that matters confidential to the SMT were not made public. He had a duty to protect individual members of staff who might be the subject of discussion. (Such a solicitous and caring leader! So we're only going to get the authorised version with the names of the guilty expunged.)

Mr Arrowsmith said that he thought the SMT was too big in any case. In his long experience no member of the SMT had ever disagreed with the head at a full staff meeting. In the light of this he was somewhat surprised that the head had not co-opted all the staff on to the SMT. (Good old Fred! At least there's a certain light and airy freedom once you've made it clear that you're a kamikaze fighter pilot.) The head replied that on the contrary he was giving serious consideration to flattening the management structure in the school which might well result in the rather slimmer SMT which Mr Arrowsmith had appeared to favour in his opening sentence. (At this point it was evident from the rapidly paling complexions of some of our self-proclaimed 'middle managers' that this was definitely one item that had not already been discussed by the SMT magic circle.) The head then wondered aloud whether the proliferation of departments and departmental heads hadn't led to excessive fragmentation and the diminution of a whole-school ethos. (Oh, oh. Some of the robber barons must have been caught using their own initiatives. I wonder which of them are for the chop?) Ms Sorenson ventured the opinion that not all the fashionable trends in industrial management practice were readily transferable to schools. (As the first known exception to Fred Arrowsmith's rule of SMT acquiescence she must think she's potentially on the hit list.) The head retorted in terms which implied that if it was good enough for Rover it would be OK for

Sludgeville as far as he was concerned. He suggested to Ms Sorenson that we shouldn't put our own vested interests before the good of the school as a whole. If we did decide to move to a Faculty structure, there would be winners as well as losers. (From the ominous tone to his voice at that point it's clear that she's on the hit list now even if she wasn't before.)

That also finished off the potential rebellion from the HODs. It's divide and rule yet again. What a weak-kneed bunch they are. So it's definitely going to happen. The only questions are when and why? Perhaps he's negotiating a new financial package with the Governors in which he trades in a few HOD scalps for a hefty raise for himself?) The head then declared that we had spent enough time on this item and that we needed to move on to the next business. (That's the usual way he cuts things dead just when they're getting interesting. I assume that this brief exchange will later be claimed as full consultation with the staff as a whole when he wants some cover for his hatchet work.)

The minutes end as follows:

8. Any Other Business.

By this time the staff had been bludgeoned into insensibility. There was only a somewhat pathetic attempt by Ms Sorenson to reinstate herself in the head's good books by proposing a vote of congratulation to him on his recent appointment to serve on the Government Task Force on Human Resource Management in Schools. (This means you will see even less of him around the place. That is something of a mixed blessing. At least you will have some respite from his bullying and interfering, but when he does deign to drop in he will continue to bawl out everyone within sight for what has been done in his absence.)

There was (surprise, surprise) no vote of thanks to yours truly on the fact that this was the last time I would be acting as clerk to the meeting. This is partly what prompted me to present you all with this my last will and testament. I could say that it has been a privilege to act in this capacity over more years than I care to remember, but on the other hand I want to avoid on this occasion the usual cant and hypocrisy, so why should I lie? In fact I would like to put on record my contempt for the majority of the lickspittles who will be reading this, and in particular for the man who has made us all what we are today.

APPRAISAL: THE PIG'S EAR APPROACH

Appraisal interviews are now a compulsory feature of the education service in England and Wales. Numerous guides on how to conduct such interviews are appearing on the market, but many appraisers of my acquaintance appear to have been following a different set of instructions. I have now managed to trace the source of their time-dishonoured techniques. This DIY Appraisal Manual appears to assume, for some reason, that the appraiser will generally be a male headteacher and the appraisee a young female teacher. It reads as follows:

1.0 Before the interview.
1.1 Forget that this is appraisal interview day and that you are due to interview 'Jenny Jones' first. This farcical charade has been imposed upon you anyway, so it's not surprising you should resent the whole damned waste of time.

1.2 Make sure you are doing something vitally important as far as you are concerned when she arrives.

1.3 Signal her to take a seat in front of your desk once she has explained why she is here.

1.4 Ignore her for a few minutes while you finish off the job you're doing.

1.5 Have no documents to hand concerning Jenny Jones.

1.6 Better still, have no documents anywhere concerning Jenny Jones. (Under no circumstances should your staff have job descriptions - that simply encourages the barrack room lawyers. Written records of the appraisals of previous years could be used in evidence against you. Put nothing in writing. Destroy any records kept by your misguided predecessor.)

1.7 Don't have any known performance criteria circulating around the workplace. (Keeping employees in the dark also keeps them on their toes. Letting them know what to expect may give some of them the edge.)

2.0 At the start of the interview

2.1 Stay behind your desk. (Reminding your staff of your authority over them never does any harm. It's your office. Let them know it.)

2.2 If Jenny says she has produced a self-evaluation in preparation for the interview, tell her that's OK if that sort of thing turns her on but it wasn't necessary as you prefer to retain a certain degree of spontaneity of these occasions. (On no account should you offer to read self-evaluations. You are not concerned about the introspective ramblings of your subordinates. Let them produce poetry or novels if they are seeking therapy through writing.)

2.3 Address her throughout as Ms Jones. (There is no recommended standard pronunciation for 'Ms', but you can, with practice learn to enunciate it with the faintest suggestion of an amused sneer. This should put the feminists in their place.)

2.4 Say you can't remember what the two of you agreed last year and ask her what she can recall.

2.5 Brush aside any recollections she claims to have and propose starting again with a clean slate.

2.6 Don't negotiate any agreed agenda for the interview. (Never let them know what's likely to come next. Whatever it is, you've decided it and it's non-negotiable.)

3.0 During the interview.

3.1 Don't use mealy-mouthed terms such as staff development, individual performance or even appraisal to describe the interview you are conducting. You know, because the Minister of State for Education has publicly said so, that this is all about teacher assessment and that this will ultimately be linked to such things as staff salary levels etc. So make sure they are also aware of it.

3.2 Avoid open-ended questions at all costs. (These are only an invitation to the interviewees to ramble on about what's on their minds. Remember it's not what's on their minds, but what's on your mind that matters.)

3.3 Closed questions are better because they usually only require yes or no answers. Insist on her providing a yes or a no. You want to know clearly where she stands on the issues that concern you.

3.4 Leading questions are better still because you are giving her a sure indication of the kind of response that you want. If she doesn't provide those responses, then more fool her.

3.5 Best of all - avoid questions altogether and simply make a series of statements. This may be the one chance in the year that you have to put her straight on your key concerns. A monologue is much better than a dialogue for such purposes.

3.6 Concentrate on how you have rated her over the last year. Don't bother too much about the year to come. That's far too airy-fairy at this point in time. You can deal with that in next year's interview. Always remember the adage: "Better retrospective than prospective."

3.7 Answer the telephone when it rings. You might miss a trick or two if you ask the caller to ring back later. Anyway she might like the chance to mull over some of the home truths you have just been imparting to her.

3.8 Be as judgmental as possible. Stress any of her personality defects of which you are aware. Personality is far more important than performance. (Keep some Kleenex handy in case of tears. You don't want her blubbing all over your things.)

3.9 If you are aware of any failings over the last year, then be as punitive as possible. It's no good letting her think she can get away with mistakes scot-free.

3.10 If you have no direct evidence of any errors of judgment etc. then rely on hearsay evidence. (You haven't got the time to go round wet-nursing all your subordinates.) There must be somebody in the organisation who doesn't like her and is prepared to spread the poison. Don't tell her who is dishing the dirt on her. That way you protect your sources and give her little chance of discounting their allegations. (This also has the general effect of making your staff suspicious of each other. 'Divide and rule' is as powerful a management precept as ever it was.)

3.11 It's best if you've given no indication at any time during the year that you were in any way dissatisfied with her work. That way it will come as a complete surprise to her during the interview and she will be less likely to have some cock and bull defence story ready.

3.12 If she does try to tell her side of the story, jump down her throat immediately. She's bound to try and justify herself isn't she?

3.13 If she comes the old sob story about the difficulties of her job, tell her at some length what a lousy job you've got. Imply it isn't made any easier by having to deal with people like her.

3.14 If she goes into a sullen sulk, then let her. Certainly don't bother to try to discover if there are any hidden agendas she is reluctant to come out with. That's far too tiresome and tedious a process.

3.15 If she still persists in putting forward ideas she has about her job, try the 'yes, but' technique. She'll soon get the message that her suggestions are impractical and that she's wasting your time. It's highly unlikely that she will have anything worth paying attention to anyway. Remember you're not there to listen. You're in charge, not her. Don't let her forget it.

3.16 Don't ask her if she feels she's had any successes over the last year. If she suggests herself that she has had some achievements then simply say that you should damn well hope she has. That's what she's paid for after all.

3.17 If she has the gall to query why she's been passed over for promotion yet again, don't, whatever you do, give her the real reasons; no matter how tempted you might be to do so. There are those stupid Equal Opportunities people who could make things awkward even if you did deny you'd ever said any such thing. Just say you're flabbergasted she should put that question after all you've said already. (Chances are she'll have a baby soon anyway and pack the job in. There's not much gratitude around these days with young women.)

3.18 Ask her to see who's knocking at your door. Attend to whoever is calling. They can't be any less important than she is.

4.0 At the end of the interview.

4.1 You decide when you've had enough.

4.2 Don't agree any specific, concrete targets with her for the coming year. (See 1.6, 1.7 and 3.6 above.)

4.3 Don't bother about identifying any staff development needs she may have. (Why waste precious resources on someone you don't think will stay with you for long anyway? In any case you know that development training is usually a waste of time. After all you didn't need any training to be an appraiser, did you?)

4.4 Don't write down any conclusions or ask her to sign any agreed record of the outcomes. She might refuse and ask for an independent assessment from some higher authority.

4.5 Just tell her to pull her socks up next year or else.

4.6 Ask her to send the next interviewee in, whoever it is.

THE BAD CONFERENCE-GOER'S GUIDE

In what now seems like a long life-time of organisation and attendance, I have come across a fair number of participants who seem determined that they, and anyone else unfortunate enough to cross their path, should derive the minimum possible benefit from education conferences. This is bad enough, but what really worries me about these characters is that somewhere, somehow, they are presumably 'educating' others. In the hope of pricking some consciences, therefore, I offer the following guidelines to bad participation at conferences.

● When choosing your conference, don't bother about the subject matter. It's the desirability or otherwise of the venue that should influence your decision. You're not exactly looking for expert advice on Special Educational Needs, but if there's a conference on that subject lined up for Cannes, and someone is fool enough to pay your expenses, you go squire.

● When you apply for the conference, say you'll pay on arrival. If the conference organisers insist on prior payment, simply ignore them. If the final demand letter says no prepayment, no joining instructions, then pay the minimum required in advance. Under no circumstances pay for the 'extras' for social events. (See the later section on "gatecrashing".)

● If the conference organisers ask you to complete forms in advance, either ignore them or fill them in a totally cavalier fashion: it doesn't really matter which seminars or workshops you sign up for, you can always change your mind when you get there.

● The only thing you need to read in advance is where and when the conference is taking place: you don't have to bother about the rest of the bumf, there'll always be spare copies when you arrive.

● Under no circumstances should you agree to be involved in the conference organisation or agree to take on any of those thankless chores like chairing seminars etc. There's always some other poor sucker who'll take on those responsibilities. You're there to take not to give.

● When making your travel arrangements for distant conferences see if you can cadge a lift in someone else's car, but don't forget to claim for first class rail travel at the least.

● If the conference is near home, don't bother with overnight stays at the conference centre. Just attend the sessions you're interested in and go straight back home. There's nothing to be gained by involving yourself in the general life of the conference on occasions like these.

● If you have to drive to the conference yourself, don't worry about parking. There'll always be some spare place marked "Disabled" or "Conference Organisers". Sometimes they place the odd traffic cone in such spots. Stick it in the boot. You never know when it might come in handy.

● If you haven't paid already, try going through registration without signing any cheques. This is easier if you're abroad and can claim not to understand the language or these strange foreign procedures. If they press you, try the "I'm a guest of the conference organisers" line. Only cough up if they threaten you with deportation.

● When they give you a badge with your name on, put it in your pocket, and just show it when coming in and going out, and then only if they've got security procedures and the like. You don't want to go ruining your clothes by fixing badges on. You'll have your business cards to give to anyone who's important or worth nobbling. The others don't matter anyway as far as knowing your name's concerned.

● If you've got mates at the conference, stick with your own clique most of the time. If you do mix at all make sure it's with the people who matter. Never waste your time on idle chit chat with the common herd. The real trick is to be in with the exclusive clique you know everybody else would like to join.

● If there are any business meetings avoid them like the plague. All those boring elections and the like! And there's always the offchance that you'll be asked to do something which might give you the embarrassment of having to turn it down in public. If by any chance you do get roped into a business meeting then raise some obscure and obstructive point of order that ties them up in knots. They'll be glad to get shot of you.

● If you want to get yourself listed as having given a paper (looks good on the old CV!), don't bother meeting any deadlines for its production set by the organisers. Deadlines aren't deadly any more! Simply turn up with a copy on the day and insist on it being duplicated and circulated. You don't have to bother to turn up and deliver it as long as the title is registered as part of the conference proceedings. For the same reason the quality of the paper doesn't really matter either unless you're also looking to publication. Just make sure you've thought up a snappy title.

● Try to grab as many papers by others as you can lay your hands on. Take a few spares in every case. They can always produce a few more if they run out. If a paper you want isn't available complain immediately to the organisers and demand one.

● Complaining about most things usually improves the service. A few good grumbles will keep the conference organisers on their toes. If you complain loudly enough about the accommodation or the quality of the food you might be able to get a refund - that's assuming you've paid in the first place.

● Certainly don't pay for any official dinners and the like. Far too pricey. If you can't gatecrash these events, and you want to hear the after dinner speaker, just barge in after the meal.

● Don't bother to turn up on time for lectures and the like.

There'll always be a few seats left after they've started even if they are in the middle of a row. Get out before the end so you're the first in line for the coffee queue.

● Don't hesitate about interrupting the speakers if you can spot a mistake they've made. It'll just show how smart you are. If you don't feel like a public intervention, try voicing your criticisms to your neighbour, preferably loudly enough for the speaker to hear anyway. After the seminar you should invariably damn the speaker with faint praise or alternatively praise the speaker with faint damns. This also demonstrates to all and sundry just how clued up you are in this field.

● If they try that trick of getting the participants in seminars to contribute their thoughts, keep your lips firmly buttoned as far as your own creative thoughts are concerned but pick up any ideas you can steal from others. On the other hand there's never anything to be lost by bragging about the wonderful things that you've achieved back at work, particularly if these miracles bear no relation to reality. This is known as 'conference-speak'.

● If you decide to pass up on some part of the conference, ask for a refund on your conference fee. A lot depends on the weather during the conference as to how much you're going to attend anyway. That beach down the road looks awfully inviting.

THE CHRISTMAS CARD AS A WEAPON IN MANAGEMENT WARFARE

In my schoolteaching youth I once joined the staff of a school ruled over, and I use the term advisedly, by an exceptionally autocratic and devious headteacher. In her attitudes towards consultation and participation she made Catherine the Great seem like a precursor of the Russian democratic movement. I remember that during my first term in the school one of the old lags took me aside and gave me some sound advice on how to survive in the trench warfare that passed for inter-personal relations in the outfit. The final words were something to the effect of: "Oh, and don't forget to send her a Christmas card. She sends one to every member of staff."

Towards the end of the Autumn term I deposited my card in her in-tray in good time. When no card came back in return, I began to worry whether I had been conned into fetching the equivalent of the bucket of steam that all apprentices are requested to find by their elders and betters. But no. Lo and behold; on something like the 23rd of December her Christmas card duly appeared through the post at my home address bearing tidings of good cheer to all mankind.

It was only then that I fully realised the potential for using the Christmas card as an attacking move to which no reactive defence could be effective in the game of management chess. For just consider. If I had not been forewarned and had not already anticipated the move, I would have been stuck two days before Christmas with a card to which I could make no response that did not leave me in checkmate. I did not know her address and she was ex-directory so the telephone book was no help. Even if I had managed to contact one of the few trusties who knew her present whereabouts, I could be sure that my feeble attempts at a Sicilian defence would be reported widely, and in any case it was most unlikely that any card I sent at that late stage would get there by the due date.

When I returned to school the next term and checked with the others, I discovered that they all received her cards around Christmas Eve or the 23rd at the earliest, so the timing was precise. To return to the military metaphor, the missile was launched at the precise moment when it could wreak maximum havoc in the defences of the unsuspecting recipients. From then on, the new member of staff was wrong-footed into a guilty posture as someone who had failed to share the glad tidings of the Yuletide season. This would have made me the equivalent of one of those few diehards who refused to take part in the Christmas truce game of football between the enemy trenches in the Great War. Most of the school's battle-weary veterans had, of course, made their pre-emptive strikes by sending their cards earlier, but this was really only an exercise in damage limitation because she then had the satisfaction of knowing that she had again forced many who had borne her little but ill-will for many a blood-soaked decade into a monstrous act of such dreadful hypocrisy that their psyches were scarred for yet another year. This was only one of many missiles which this headteacher used to such deadly effect but I had to admire this particularly ruthless use of the Christmas card as what amounted to the Stealth Bomber of its time.

Since that time I have made careful observations of the exchange of poison pen Christmas cards and I am now in a position to make a definitive report on the art. (By the way, if anyone reading this had previously been under the impression that Christmas cards between colleagues were tokens of good will, then I can only assume that he or she has the kind of good-hearted naïveté which renders the possessor unfit for the cut and thrust of management warfare.)

The headteacher who wants to save on the kind of postage bill which must have been incurred by the lady I referred to above, but still wishes to cause mayhem in the ranks, simply puts one card on the staff noticeboard which says: "With thanks for your support this past year. To all the staff but one. From Mary." Nobody can then be certain that he or she has not been rumbled at last. Guilt will be struck into many a craven heart and cruel witch-hunts will be instigated by those who wish to move suspicion from themselves. The only defect with this gambit is that the private residence of the headteacher is unlikely to be full to the gunnels with the Christmas cards forced out of a reluctant staff which the first lady I referred to could display to unsuspecting visitors as evidence of the high regard in which she was held by her devoted team of toiling pedagogues. This can be remedied by displaying annually re-usable cards on which the head in question has forged suitably nauseating messages of obsequious tribute from colleagues many of whom may now be long dead in any case. (This is known to aficionados as the Beau Geste strategem.)

Those who have left one set of trenches to move to another section of the battlefield can cause much collateral damage by sending a card to their former fellow infantry with a suitable message. One specimen I especially admired went as follows: "To all the inmates. Sitting in my private office in front of my personal Apple Mac computer, I am thinking of you all in cell block H. Merry Christmas and a Happy New Year. Fred." This particular character was probably still using a quill pen in a staff room designed for 20 and used by 50, but his shell-shocked former colleagues would inevitably conclude that they were alone in being singled out to work in hell-hole front line conditions.

There is an art also in obtaining cards from the great and the good. These are usually massive embossed affairs paid for by the various quangos which they head and they are bound to impress your guests with your contacts in high places. To obtain such cards there is no need to send anything similar yourself. As long as you post early to anyone of eminence who had the misfortune to cross your path at some point in your earlier existences, it does not really matter how cheap your own card appears. Indeed, a card with a hideous design bearing the note: "All proceeds to the orphans of the People's Front for the Liberation of Turbestan" is entirely suitable, because the dignitary concerned may still harbour some residual feelings of guilt at having ditched all the non-establishment causes he or she once espoused. Sending off one of the quango's best at the expense of the taxpayer is a small price to pay for easing one's conscience.

While we are on the subject of 'charity' cards, do not underestimate the fund-raising potential of your school having its own official card. The award of a prize of a box of crayons for the pupil who submits the best design should ensure that you do not have to commission a professional artist at high expense and the pupils can also be relied upon to persuade their parents to purchase boxfulls of the cards, however awful they may be, on the grounds that it is the only way you will ever be able to afford to mend the leaking roof over the hall. You can then send these cards through the school post to such of the local citizenry you consider appropriate. School governors, in particular, should receive theirs together with an invitation to the Christmas Carol Concert to be held in the school hall (weather permitting).

Under no circumstances should you, as a headteacher, ever send a card to a member of staff which is bigger than the one sent to you, unless you are employing the scatter gun technique referred to at the start of this chapter. Under normal circumstances, then, it is essential to wait until you receive a card before you reciprocate. This can cause problems because some members of staff will creep in any time before the 25th to leave a card on your desk, thus ensuring that you are aware that they are in school during holidays. Far from giving them a gold star for this, make sure the card you send in return is appreciably smaller than the one you received, and leave it in their in-tray dated the day after you received theirs.

Christmas cards are an excellent means of demonstrating your contempt for your colleagues. Always send, for example, in response to those secular greetings from known atheists and agnostics on the staff, cards which depict the virgin mother and child and contain messages offering everlasting salvation to those who truly believe. To the shrinking minority who are still active churchgoers you should send examples of those profane 'joke' cards which are now beginning to proliferate. For overseas colleagues in the far off colonies such as Australia and Canada, who will not be expecting a card from you, post your cards sometime in early April so that they arrive by overland camel train sometime in mid-December. This ensures that they have to reply by airmail at considerable expense. Central and Eastern Europe offer unrivalled opportunities this year for addressing your cards in such a way that they offend practically everybody. Make sure your colleagues in the Ukraine receive cards with the Union of Soviet Socialist Republics on the envelopes in underlined capital letters. Any cards to St Petersburg should be addressed to Petrograd, thereby also annoying the Leningrad faction. But the possibilities are endless once you have grasped the essential message of the true purpose of sending Christmas cards.

So a Merry Christmas and a Happy New Year to all my readers but two.